Table

Preface

The purpose of this book is to reach out to young adult believers in Jesus Christ who are about to enter, or are already attending college and offer guidance for their time in school. I am hopeful that anyone of any age or stage in life who reads this book will find it enlightening and encouraging.

If perchance you have opened this book but do not know Jesus Christ as your personal Savior, please consider the following. Suppose you need a car. You must choose between four cars—three are priced at $25,000 and the fourth car is free. Which would you check out first? Of course it would be the free one. Suppose you investigate all four of them and find the free one to be by far the best car. The choice would be easy!

The choice of trusting Christ as your personal Savior is similar. All other religions of the world ask you to pay in some way. The offer of salvation from Christ is totally free, based on faith alone in the sacrificial work He accomplished on the cross on our behalf. The offer is not only eternal life in heaven, but also for what Christ called "life more abundantly" while on this earth. He offers us His joy—peace that transcends all understanding.

My prayer is that you will trust in the finished work of Christ on the cross for your salvation, freeing you from the penalty of your sin. Jesus is the only way, and He will be faithful to keep you eternally secure in Him. If you have not trusted Christ as your Savior and still have questions about God and His Word, I hope you approach this book and its message with an open mind. It is written for all who are seeking honest answers. God has not hidden Himself; if you seek Him, He will be found.

Chapter 1

Reason or Faith?

"Modern culture is not altogether opposed to the gospel. But it is out of all connection with it. It not only prevents the acceptance of Christianity. It prevents Christianity even from getting a hearing."

- J. Gresham Machen

Should Christians Reason for the Truth?

Is it even possible to reach the truth about Jesus Christ and Christianity through reasoning? Is Christianity only accepted by faith that is apart from reason? This chapter will address these questions.

God created all humans in His image, and this image includes the ability to reason. Consider Genesis 1:27: "So God created man in His own image." Jude 10 tells us, "Indeed, it is by reasoning that humans are distinguished from brute beasts."

God created us with the ability to reason and he wants us to *use* reason! Isaiah 1:18: "'Come now, and let us *reason* together,' says the Lord, 'Though your sins are like scarlet, they shall be as white as snow; though they are red like crimson, they shall be as wool.'"

Paul also used reasoning as described in Acts 17:2-3: "As was his custom, Paul went into the synagogue, and on three Sabbath days he reasoned with them from the Scriptures, explaining and proving that the Messiah had to suffer and rise from the dead. 'This Jesus I am proclaiming to you is the Messiah.'" Paul knew that the truth claims of the Bible are reasonable and logically defensible.

1 Peter 3:15 tells us to be ready to give answers. "But in your hearts revere Christ as Lord. Always be prepared to give an answer to everyone who asks you to give the reason for the hope that you have. But do this with gentleness and respect."

The Greek word for answer is "apologia." It doesn't mean to apologize, but is a legal term meaning to give an answer, an organized defense, or a reasoned response to a charge or accusation in a court of law. The command is used in the form of a present active imperative—*continually* be prepared to give a reason for what you believe.

This defense of the Christian faith is the field of theology known as "apologetics." Apologists defend the truth claims of the Christian faith as revealed in the Bible, using evidence, facts, and reasonable logic. Apologists also unmask the inconsistencies and irrationality of opposing truth claims. The two-fold purpose of the study of apologetics is to: 1) confirm the rationality of their beliefs to believers and 2) give reasonable answers to questions and doubts that prevent unbelievers from accepting the truth claims of the Bible and Jesus Christ.

In Philippians 1:7b, Paul describes his mission as "...in the defense [apologia] and confirmation of the Gospel." 2 Corinthians 10:5 tells us, "We demolish arguments and every pretension that sets itself up against the knowledge of God, and we take captive every thought to make it obedient to Christ."

Jude 3 presents the mandate to reason for our faith: "Beloved, when I gave all diligence to write unto you of the common salvation, it was needful for me to write unto you, and exhort you that you should earnestly contend for the faith which was once delivered unto the saints." Jude wanted to write a more pleasant letter about our salvation, but false teachers and heretics had perverted the gospel. Jude tells us we are not to be passive in response to false teachers, but defenders of the true gospel of Christ.

In the Old Testament, the Israelites (God's chosen people) battled against flesh-and-blood enemies. Today, His representatives (Church Age believers) are contending against more powerful and deceptive enemies: Satan and his demon warriors. We see this in Ephesians 6:12: "For we do not wrestle against flesh and blood, but against principalities, against powers, against the rulers of the darkness of this age, against spiritual hosts of wickedness in the heavenly places." We as believers must learn how to "give answers" and "contend earnestly for the faith." We must expose Satan's lies and the illogical and irrational strategies used by his false teachers, while showing the truth claims of the Bible are reasonable.

You can't argue people into faith in Jesus. Apologetics isn't arguing; it is answering honest questions and reasoning through any doubts that prevent acceptance of the truth of Christianity and the claims of Jesus Christ.

C.S. Lewis, novelist and Christian apologist, notes that, "...nearly everyone I know who has embraced Christianity in adult life has been influenced by what seemed to him to be at least a probable argument for theism." Lewis was an atheist who came to Christ when challenged by apologetic reasoning.

What is faith? Is it reasonable?

Many people, including some Christians, believe that faith and reason are polar opposites. In his time, Mark Twain defined faith as "believing what you know ain't true." Sam Harris, a philosopher and neuroscientist, once said, "Faith is the license religious people give themselves to keep believing when reasons fail." In the documentary "Religulous," comedian and political commentator Bill Maher says, "Faith means making a virtue out of not thinking." Evolutionary biologist Richard Dawkins states, "The whole point of religious faith, its strength and chief glory, is that it does not depend on rational justification."

These men assume that faith excludes reason, and since Christianity is affirmed by faith, using reason to assess the truth of Christianity is impossible. We will show these assumptions to be false.

The Bible defines "faith" in Hebrews 11:1: "Now faith is the substance of things hoped for, the evidence of things not seen." Faith is looking at all the available evidence and reaching the most reasonable conclusion based on that evidence.

A detective follows the evidence left behind of things not presently seen. God has left evidence for His unseen existence in the heavens. Psalm 19:1-2: "The heavens declare the glory of God; the skies proclaim the work of his hands. Day after day they pour forth speech; night after night they reveal knowledge." Job 12:7-9 describes the evidence God left for us in the created world: "But ask the animals, and they will teach you, or the birds in the sky, and they will tell you; or speak to the earth, and it will teach you, or let the fish in the sea inform you. Which of all these does not know that the hand of the Lord has done this?" Romans 1:20 tells us, "For since the creation of the world God's invisible qualities—his eternal power and divine nature—have been clearly seen, being understood from what has been made, so that people are without excuse."

God left His fingerprints on His creation; it is up to us to use this general revelation (the evidence He has revealed) to reason for the truth claims of the Bible—His written Word and special revelation. Christians are called to use their God-given ability to reason in order to come to the conclusion that God is real.

Unbelievers and believers look at the same evidence of what happened in the past and come to different conclusions about how it happened. However, both require at least some faith to believe that their version of unseen past events is the truth. Faith in God isn't unreasonable.

Noted Christian apologist Craig Hazen, PhD, explains this point: "We have got to start talking differently about 'faith.' Unfortunately, we have let the secular world and antagonists like Bill Maher define the term for us. What they mean by 'faith' is blind leaping. That is what they think our commitment to Christ and the Christian view of the world is all about. They think we have simply disengaged our minds and leapt blindly into the religious abyss. The biblical view of saving Christian faith has never had anything to do with blind leaping. Jesus himself was fixed

13

on the idea that we can know the truth—and not just in some spiritual or mystical way. Rather, he taught that we can know the truth about God, humans, and salvation objectively. That is, the very best forms of investigation, evidence, and careful reasoning will inevitably point to God and His great plans for us."

Philosophical Truth

Christian apologist Dr. Ravi Zacharias, in his book The End of Reason (p. 117), describes how a person arrives at a philosophical truth in the same way a detective does. He says that all philosophical truth will have: 1) logical consistency, 2) empirical adequacy, and 3) experiential relevance.

The first test, logical consistency, considers whether an idea is logical or illogical, in other words, whether it make sense. If it is illogical, it can be presumed the idea is wrong, but just because an idea is logical does not mean it is true. The second test is empirical adequacy. Is there enough supporting evidence for the idea to become a believable model? Finally, there is the issue of experiential relevance. Is the model consistent with past experience? If the model cannot explain the evidence and does not pass these three tests, it is time to drop it and seek another.

Historical Science

Detectives, and anyone else who tries to determine what happened anytime in the past, use historical science rather than the scientific method, since a past event cannot be reproduced for observation. It is important to understand the difference between historical and observational / operational science.

Observational science uses the scientific method on observable and measurable phenomena. Historical science looks at evidence left behind from the past to figure out how this evidence came to be as it is now observed. This type of scientific inquiry occurs in cosmology, astronomy, astrophysics, geology, paleontology, biology, and archaeology. Science classes may not distinguish between the two methods, but there clearly is an important distinction.

Historical science asks questions like: What happened? What caused this event or that natural feature to arise? When and how did this happen?

Since historical models cannot be reproduced to be tested by the scientific method, the conclusions reached will necessarily contain a certain level of assumption that can trigger doubt. This is the reason juries are only required to convict a suspect based on belief beyond a reasonable doubt, not beyond a shadow of all doubt. A guilty verdict must be reasonable, logical, and consistent with all observed evidence that the suspect committed the crime. That is the highest level of certainty that can be achieved about an event without seeing it happen.

John H. Horner, a well-known paleontologist, confirms this in his book <u>Dinosaur Lives</u> (p. 19): "...paleontology (the branch of science concerned with fossil animals and plants) is a historical science, a science based on circumstantial evidence, after the fact. We can never

15

reach hard and fast conclusions in our study of ancient plants and animals....These days it's easy to go through school for a good many years, sometimes even through college, without ever hearing that some sciences are historical or by nature inconclusive."

As a homicide detective, I learned the appropriate process for using evidence to come to a conclusion about a past event. A detective must first observe the circumstantial evidence left behind at the crime scene. He or she uses reason and logic to determine the likely circumstances that brought the evidence to where it was found and then uses forensic science to investigate it and hopefully show how it points to a suspect. The detective obtains direct evidence from all people claiming to be witnesses to the crime. Without any prior assumptions or agenda, the detective interviews witnesses and determines if that testimony is consistent with the physical or circumstantial evidence. A witness must be trustworthy, so an ethical detective will match the known evidence with the witness' statement.

Evidence rightly examined does not lie; however, witnesses *have* been known to lie. From those observations, the detective forms a philosophical conclusion, or scenario, of what happened. This is called a "model" by science—a conclusion about an unobserved past event reached through logical reasoning. The resulting conclusions are, in fact, philosophical conclusions.

A detective follows where the evidence leads with an open mind, with no prior assumptions, and without omitting any evidence that does not support his model.

A Lie Prevents One from Trusting Christ

Reasoning can be used in the spiritual world too. Consider this example of how a lie can prevent an individual from trusting Christ as Savior. At a banquet I was seated across from a young man from China. He was a chemical engineer who had moved to Houston to work for a petrochemical company. As we conversed, it became obvious that he was not a believer in Christ. I eventually turned the conversation into a spiritual discussion. I was able to present the plan of salvation, which he acknowledged he understood. After I completed my gospel message, I asked him if he was ready to trust in Christ as his personal Savior. He responded that he was not ready. I asked what was holding him back. He responded, "Evolution."

He was being perfectly honest with me—he had been indoctrinated in communist China with the theory of Darwinian evolution. He had been told that evolution disproves the possibility of the existence of God. (Evolution can be classified as a "pretension that sets itself up against the knowledge of God," and we are commanded "to demolish arguments and take them captive," as stated above in 2 Corinthians 10:5.)

I did my best to show the young man why Darwinian evolution was a lie and why God was the only explanation for the evidence all around us in heaven and on earth. Unfortunately, he was not ready to hear the evidence. I gave him a copy of an excellent book by Norman Geisler and Frank Turek, I Don't Have Enough Faith to be an Atheist. To accept the Darwinian evolution model as fact requires a tremendous amount of faith. Evolution does not explain the evidence, as we will see!

Frank Pastore Comes to Faith

Frank Pastore attended a Catholic school where he was taught Darwinian evolution as a fact. He did not believe in God at that time. He went on to become a Major League baseball player. Several fellow players were Christians and had repeatedly given him the gospel message. However, these teammates could not answer the many questions he had about God, so he rejected their message.

Frank had a career-ending injury in 1987 after about eight years in baseball. Soon after the injury he went to a cookout with some Christian players where he met a leader from a Christian athletic organization. When asked if he believed in God, Frank cited the reasons he did not believe in God. The leader did not have an answer right then but instead gave him three books: Mere Christianity by C. S. Lewis, Scientific Creationism by Henry Morris, and Evidence That Demands a Verdict by Josh McDowell. The Christian leader asked Frank to read these books and come back and tell him where they were wrong.

Frank read through all the books and chose to trust Christ as his personal Savior. He described his two subsequent emotions: first, joy in knowing his sins were forgiven. But second, he was angry because he realized he had been told a lie through his entire life. He now knew that naturalistic evolution, secular humanism, and other atheistic ideologies were myths and that Christianity was not a myth, but the truth. He told his Christian teammates they were disobeying God in not being able to answer his questions. He went on to teach them what he had learned from the books.

Frank eventually went through seminary and, in 2004, became the host of The Frank Pastore Show on the radio in Los Angeles, which became the largest Christian talk show in the United States. He once said, "Christians are not against people or the world. But we are against false ideas that hold good people captive." Along with Ellen Vaughn, he wrote Shattered: Struck Down, But Not Destroyed. Frank was a valiant warrior for Christ until his death in 2012.

Lies that Pull People from the Church

Other lies pull believers away from their Christian walk and prevent them from advancing. Billy Graham's autobiographical book, Just as I Am, illustrates this scenario. Chuck Templeton was a fellow evangelist and Rev. Graham's very good friend. Together they had travelled the world, working alongside each other preaching the gospel. Templeton later left the ministry in order to obtain his Ph.D. from Princeton Seminary, thinking this doctoral degree would make him a more effective tool in service to the Lord. Templeton unfortunately left Princeton Seminary with a doctoral degree but an atheist's heart.

Templeton met with Rev. Graham after his graduation and revealed his "crisis of faith." Templeton had been taught in seminary that there are serious problems with the Bible and the Christian faith. Templeton told Graham the Bible contained a number of contradictions as well as several unscientific and historically inaccurate statements. These contradictions, along with the problem of evil in the world, led Templeton away from the Christian faith.

Often children who are raised in Bible-believing churches go away to college and begin to reject the Christian faith. Seven in ten Protestants age 18 to 30, both evangelical and mainstream, who attend church regularly in high school, quit attending by age 23, according to a survey by Life Way Research. I believe this is because they believe many of the lies that I confront in this book.

The truth is the Bible does not have all the problems that Templeton had been led to believe. As we will see, the Bible does correspond with science and has never been in contradiction with any scientific law. The Bible is historically accurate and has never been proven to be historically untrue. The Bible does not contradict itself in any way. Sadly, the lies posited by Templeton's seminary professors are still being told and recycled today. Without ready access to evidence to counter these lies, Templeton turned away from his faith.

My Encounter with Apologetics

I use myself as an example of a believer who became enthusiastic about our Christian faith after being exposed to the arguments for God. I had been a believer in Jesus Christ since childhood and had even been faithful in going to church, spreading the gospel, and handing out gospel tracts. And yet those I reached out to would tell me that nobody in their right mind would believe these things.

I thought the best argument we Christians had was found in the classic hymn that stated "you ask me how I know He lives, He lives within my heart." That may be true for you, but it is meaningless to an unbeliever.

This all changed around 1998 when a friend gave me an audio CD from Christian apologist Ravi Zacharias. I heard that there was evidence for God, both philosophical and scientific! I then became more confident that God was real. I was challenged—now I should start living more like God wanted me to. Doors opened for me to teach and as I shared the gospel, I started to see results. I listened to everything I could from Ravi and moved on to listen to other great apologists. I went on to do doctoral work in apologetics and have committed my life to helping others see that God's Word is truth.

Whether we know it or not, Christians are in a very important conflict. This is the age old battle of Satan versus God, the battle that started before human history began, before the fall of man in the Garden of Eden, and it is taking place today in the souls of individuals. God doesn't need spectators to watch the conflict from the sidelines; He needs warriors.

God stands ready to fortify His warriors with His truth so we can stand our ground and fight for His kingdom. In the end, Jesus Christ Himself will win the final battle. Until then, the readers of this book will receive information and methodology to use in reasoning with others and, by the power of the Holy Spirit, lead them to the truth.

Chapter Two

Why Do We Believe in God?

"God maintains a delicate balance between keeping his existence sufficiently evident so people will know he's there and yet hiding his presence enough so that people who want to choose to ignore him can do it. This way, their choice of destiny is really free."

–J.P. Moreland

Arguments for the Existence of God

Is there solid evidence that God exists? Are there logical lines of reasoning (in other words, arguments) that would lead people to conclude there is a transcendent God Who loves them?

In this chapter we will look at the top three arguments for the existence of God that are used by defenders of the faith. The existence of God is a subject of debate in philosophy and popular culture and being ready to give an answer is commanded for all believers.

The Cosmological Argument

The first argument for the existence of God is the cosmological argument. It goes like this:

1) Everything that begins to exist has a cause of its existence.
2) The universe began to exist.
3) Therefore, the universe has a cause for its existence.

This is what philosophers call a syllogism, a basic tool of logic in which a conclusion is drawn from a major premise and a minor premise. The major premise is true of the subject in general; the minor premise shares a common term with the major premise and connects a smaller part to the whole of the major premise. The conclusion shows that what is true of the whole (major premise) must be also true of the small part (minor premise).

A commonly used example of a syllogism is: All men are mortal (major premise). Socrates was a man (minor premise connected by men/ man). Therefore, Socrates was mortal (conclusion, connecting the final term to the first). The best way to argue against a syllogism is to question one or both of the premises. If you accept both premises, the conclusion is unavoidable.

Let us look at the premises of the cosmological argument. The major premise is everything that begins to exist has a cause of its existence. If something has not come into existence but does actually exist, it would have to be eternal. This argument uses what is known as the Law of Cause and Effect, or the Law/Principle of Causality. This concept was first put in writing by Greek philosopher Plato around 360 B.C. He states there must be a cause for everything that exists and every material effect must have an adequate antecedent or simultaneous cause for its existence.

The Law of Causality is very well established and accepted. No intellectually honest person would question the major premise of the cosmological argument: Everything that begins to exist has a cause of its existence.

Given that, we should closely examine the minor premise in the argument: "The universe began to exist."

What does the Bible say about this? In Genesis 1:1 the Bible states that the universe came into being: "In the beginning God created the heavens and the earth." The Hebrew word *bara* used here means a "creation from nothing." This Biblical truth is also stated in Hebrews 11:3: "By faith we understand that the universe was formed at God's command, so that what is seen was not made out of what was visible." The Bible is clear: The universe had a beginning.

Philosophically speaking, there are four possible explanations for the existence of the universe:

1) Nothing exists and all is an illusion.
2) The universe began to exist but created itself.
3) The universe is eternal and everything has always existed.
4) There was an outside source that caused the universe.

Looking at the first possibility, if "all is an illusion," then *we* are an illusion, and why would we even ask the question? Our ability to think is one proof of our existence. An illusion could not have self-consciousness or be able to think and ask questions. This possibility doesn't pass the common sense test. The world is not an illusion. If it was, and nothing is real, then it would not hurt to be hit by a truck. But it does. The first possibility is absurd, and we can dismiss it.

The second possibility is that the universe created itself and we'll address this in more depth in Chapter 5. However, common sense tells us if the universe came into being from non-existence it would need an outside agent to act upon it. Some say the laws of physics caused the universe. Yet it is also absurd to posit that the laws of physics came into existence with no outside cause or agent of cause. It is illogical to say that the universe created itself out of nothing. Nothing is "no thing"; nothing cannot do anything and nothing cannot become something. We can conclude that this is not reasonable or logical.

What about the third explanation? Is the universe eternal? The Second Law of Thermodynamics states that the amount of usable energy in the universe is declining. It also states that things go from order towards disorder. This Law points to the universe necessarily having an orderly beginning and the energy in the universe presently winding down. The third explanation is analogous to saying a car driving down the road had been driving forever. But you know that could not be the case because the engine was burning gas and the amount of gas in the car was finite. The amount of energy in the universe is finite too, so we can conclude it must have had a beginning.

That leaves us with the fourth possibility, which we'll explore in some detail below.

If the Universe Began, What Caused it?

What does science tell us about the universe and its beginning? Until theoretical physicist Albert Einstein introduced his theory of general relativity in 1916, science generally accepted the conclusion that the universe was eternal. Relativity dealt a critical blow to the idea of an eternal universe.

Einstein's mathematical calculations, based on observations, proved that the universe is not static but instead is expanding. Since it is expanding, it must have had a beginning. Einstein fully understood that his theory would be devastating to the commonly held assumption that the universe was eternal, an assumption vital to the Darwinian evolution model.

So rather than publish his research with the real numbers, Einstein fudged them in his conclusions so they did not invalidate the eternal universe model. He introduced what he called "the cosmological constant" with which he intentionally manipulated numbers so the eternal universe model would not be contradicted. When he published his work, he included the cosmological constant in his calculations without explanation.

After reading Einstein's study, mathematician Alexander Friedmann discovered the error and wrote a personal letter to Einstein pointing it out. When he did not receive a reply, which was a professional insult, Friedmann published an article in which he pointed out Einstein's error. Einstein responded by attacking Friedmann's article, but Friedmann enlisted other scholars to verify the conclusion. Friedmann's findings were proved valid by the other scholars and Einstein eventually had to apologize and admit his intentional error. Einstein is reputed to have admitted this was "the biggest blunder of my life." Science now had evidence that the universe had a beginning. Einstein concluded the universe started from a point of singularity.

In the 1920s, other scientists uncovered more evidence that the universe had a beginning. Edwin Hubble, an American astronomer, found that most galaxies display a red color or "red shift," which he believed indicate they are moving away from earth at a very high rate of speed. He believed this was evidence of an expanding universe which must have had a beginning. Hubble, too, concluded the universe started from a point of singularity.

How small is a point of singularity? The edge of a sheet of paper is about one million atoms wide. Approximately one million points of singularity can fit into the nucleus of the atom. Thus, a point of singularity is so exceedingly small, it is virtually nothing. The evidence points to the universe coming to existence from virtually nothing.

Scientists Arno Penzias and Robert Wilson, leaders of the SETI (Search for Extra-Terrestrial Intelligence) project, discovered the universe is uniformly filled with microwave radiation. This cosmic microwave background had been predicted by scientists who expected the radiation would be present as a result of the Big Bang theory. Penzias, who shared the Nobel prize for physics for the discovery of cosmic background radiation, stated, "The best data we have are exactly what I would have predicted had I nothing to go on but the first five books of Moses, the Psalms and the Bible as a whole." Penzias also concluded, "Astronomy leads us to a unique event, a universe which was created out of nothing, one with the very delicate balance needed to provide exactly the conditions required to permit life, and one which has an underlying (one might say supernatural) plan."

Scientists were not happy with this proof that the universe had a beginning. Famous British mathematician and physicist Sir Arthur Stanley Eddington said, "I find it philosophically repugnant because it did not allow evolution an infinite time to get started." Theoretical physicist Stephen Hawking made the same point: "There were therefore a number of attempts to avoid the conclusion that there had been a big bang....Many people do not like the idea that time has a beginning, probably because it smacks of divine intervention."

How Quickly did the Universe Expand?

Scientists searching the universe with microwave telescopes have reportedly found the flash from the Big Bang. They have concluded that the universe exploded at an astronomical rate—from a point of singularity to the size of the universe in a fraction of a second.

The March 2014 edition of Air and Space magazine includes an interesting article, "The Planck Telescope: News from the Dawn of Time: Will a new picture of the universe's first light overturn a theory that has reigned for 30 years?" The $900 million Planck telescope gathered much new information. In part, the article states, "These more precise measurements have narrowed the range of acceptable models explaining how the universe expanded, including models for the theory of inflation: the idea that 10^{-35} (a decimal with 35 zeros behind it then a one) second after the Big Bang, the universe expanded 100 trillion, trillion, times, from a point far smaller than an atom to something far bigger than the Milky Way....That signal—the oldest light of the cosmos stretched by the expansion of space into invisible, pervasive microwaves—has just been gathered and measured with greater precision than ever before."

This suggests what occurred at the point of creation. Scientific research performed without a preconceived assumption of an eternal universe actually matches the evidence of the Biblical witness to creation. If this information is true, the origin of our universe was much more than a Big Bang. It would be more accurate to say the Infinite Creator God spoke and it came into being.

How Big is the Universe?

The immensity of the universe is hard to imagine. Alpha Centauri, the third brightest star in the sky, is the closest star to earth at "just" 4.37 light years away. If one were to get on a space shuttle and travel at its cruising speed of 17,500 mph, which is five miles per second, it would take more than 201,000 years to reach that closest star. If someone living at the time of Jesus started traveling at that rate to the star, they would now only be 1/100th of the way there. Our Milky Way Galaxy is estimated to be approximately 100,000 light years in diameter.

Think of our solar system as the size of an American quarter coin. By this scale, the entire Milky Way Galaxy would be the size of the North American continent.

NASA scientist and agnostic Robert Jastrow, in his book, God and the Astronomers, explores the different models secular scientists use to explain how natural causes could have produced the Big Bang. He comes to this conclusion, "This is an exceedingly strange development, unexpected by all but the theologians. They have always accepted the word of the Bible: 'In the beginning God created heaven and earth.' It seems as though science will never be able to raise the curtain on the mystery of creation. For the scientist who has lived by his faith in the power of reason, the story ends like a bad dream. He has scaled the mountains of ignorance; he is about to conquer the highest peak; as he pulls himself over the final rock, he is greeted by a band of theologians who have been sitting there for centuries."

What Caused the Beginning?

The evidence is in. It is reasonable to conclude that the universe is not eternal and *did*, in fact, have a beginning. Thinking rationally beyond the first two tenets of our syllogism we can conclude that the universe must have a cause for its existence outside of itself.

Can we reach conclusions about the cause of the Big Bang by examining the effect, that is, the evidence left behind? This evidence points to a cause that is supernatural and beyond our comprehension. Professor of Philosophy Dr. William Lane Craig concludes the Cause of the universe would have these attributes: "space-less because it created space, timeless because it created time, immaterial because it created matter, infinitely powerful because it created out of nothing, infinitely intelligent because the creation event and the universe was precisely designed, personal because it made a choice to convert a state of nothing into something (impersonal forces don't make choices)." The only candidate that meets these criteria is the God of the Bible.

Some will then ask, "Who created God?" The answer has to be either that God is uncaused and eternally self-existent or He was created by an over god. If there was an over god, then the next question is who created him? The answer again would have to be another over god. This would lead to an infinite number of over gods but there would have to be an eternal god as the first cause. Yet the evidence points to the Creator God of the universe being infinite and this would not allow for an over god. The evidence points to an infinite God, as described in the Bible, as the only God.

Robert Jastrow verifies this again, as quoted in Christianity Today, August 6, 1982: "Astronomers now find they have painted themselves into a corner because they have proven, by their own methods, that the world began abruptly in an act of creation to which you can trace the seeds of every star, every planet, every living thing in this cosmos and on the earth. And they have found that all this happened as a product of forces they cannot hope to discover. That there are what I or anyone would call supernatural forces at work is now, I think, a scientifically proven fact."

It is safe to conclude that the cosmological argument is a valid rationale to determine that the cause for the universe points to the existence of the God of the Bible.

The Teleological Argument, or the Argument from Design

The teleological or design argument states that since the universe and living things exhibit consistency, unity, pattern, and a design in their order, a Designer must therefore exist. The term, "teleological," is derived from the Greek word telos, meaning "end" or "purpose." The conclusion is that the universe is the way it is because it was created by an intelligent being in order to accomplish a purpose; we can conclude the Designer had a purpose in designing.

William Paley (1743-1805), the father of the design argument, was an English clergyman and philosopher. He argued that if one found a watch on the beach it would point to a designer. Paley likens the universe to a watch, with many ordered parts working in harmony to further some purpose. Paley's logic is as follows: Human artifacts are products of intelligent design. The universe resembles human artifacts. Therefore, the universe is a product of intelligent design.

This logically leads to the question: Is there evidence for design in the universe? Could design have come from time plus chance after the Big Bang? Anyone who has worked with explosives knows that explosions do not create order, but rather disorder. Many scientists point out that the universe appears to be finely tuned and well-ordered to support life.

Atheist Stephen Hawking, in his book, A Brief History of Time, wrote, "It would be very difficult to explain why the universe should have begun in just this way, except as the act of a God who intended to create beings like us." Paul Davies, a physicist, cosmologist, and biologist tells us, "There is for me powerful evidence that there is something going on behind it all....It seems as though somebody has fine-tuned nature's numbers to make the universe....The impression of design is overwhelming."

Astronomer Dr. Fred Hoyle states, "A common sense interpretation of the facts suggests that a super intellect has monkeyed with physics, as well as with chemistry and biology, and that there are no blind forces worth speaking about in nature. The numbers one calculates from the facts seem to me so overwhelming as to put this conclusion almost beyond question."

Dr. Allan Sandage, an American astronomer notes, "It was my science that drove me to the conclusion that the world is much more complicated than can be explained by science, it is only through the supernatural that I can understand the mystery of existence."

Similarly, Dr. Walter Bradley, Professor of Mechanical Engineering at Texas A & M University, states, "Discoveries of the last half of the twentieth century have brought the scientific community to the realization that our universe and our planet in the universe are so remarkably unique that it is almost impossible to imagine how this could have happened accidentally, causing many agnostic scientists to concede that indeed some intelligent creative force may be required to account for it."

Frank Tipler, a professor of mathematical physics, examined the physical laws of the universe and reached the conclusion that there must be a God. In his book, The Physics of Immortality, he writes, "When I began my career as a cosmologist some twenty years ago, I was a convinced atheist. I never in my wildest dreams imagined that one day I would be writing a book purporting to show that the central claims of Judeo-Christian theology are in fact true, that these claims are straightforward deductions of the laws of physics as we now understand them. I have been forced into these conclusions by the inexorable logic of my own special branch of physics."

We can safely conclude that the heavens do proclaim the glory of God. The evidence points to the God of the Bible as the Creator of the design evident in the universe.

Design in Life on Earth

The universe points to a designer, but design is also evident in life on our planet. The teleological argument can be used here too. First, how did life come to be on our planet? Francis Crick, biochemist and spiritual skeptic says, "An honest man, armed with all the knowledge available to us now, could only state that in some sense, the origin of life appears at the moment to be almost a miracle, so many are the conditions which would have had to have been satisfied to get it going."

The marvels of the bodies of both animals and humans are evidently endless. Organic chemist Dr. A.E. Wilder-Smith says, "When one considers that the entire chemical information to construct a man, elephant, frog or an orchid was compressed into two minuscule reproductive cells (sperm and egg nuclei), one can only be astounded. In addition to this, all the information is available on the genes to repair the body (not only to construct it) when it is injured. If one were to request an engineer to accomplish this feat of information miniaturization, one would be considered fit for the psychiatric clinic."

Human DNA points to a designer. The human body contains around 70 trillion cells. Inside each are two str of DNA, which function like an incredibly complicated computer program. If the strands of one cell were stretched out, the chain would be more than seven feet long, but so thin it could not be seen, even with a powerful microscope. If the DNA from all the cells in a human body were connected together, the string would reach the moon and back more than a hundred times. But it would be so small that it would not fill two tablespoons. The information on the seven-foot strand of DNA in one cell would fill over four thousand pages of an encyclopedia. All the information in the 70 trillion cells in the human body reduced to pages of an encyclopedia would fill the Grand Canyon 40 times. Could this have happened by "time plus chance"? It is not reasonable to believe that.

When we allow honest science to present this type of evidence, it inevitably tells us a supernatural force is the explanation for the design of life. Only the Creator God of the Bible matches up with the evidence. Scientist John Polkinghorne concludes this of true science: "Science and religion are friends, not foes, in the common quest for knowledge. Some people may find it surprising, for there is a feeling throughout our society that religious belief is outmoded, or downright impossible, in a scientific age. I don't agree. In fact, I'd go so far as to say that if people knew a bit more about science than many of them actually do, they'd find it easier to share my view."

Mainstream science truly has a problem—its adherents are blinded by their assumptions. Richard 'ontin, an agnostic scientist, admits as much: "We take 'e of science in spite of the patent absurdity of some of its constructs, in spite of its failure to fulfill many of its extravagant promises of health and life, in spite of the tolerance of the scientific community for unsubstantiated just-so stories, because we have a prior commitment, a commitment to materialism. It is not that the methods and institutions of science somehow compel us to accept a material explanation of the phenomenal world, but, on the contrary, that we are forced by our *a priori* adherence to material causes to create an apparatus of investigation and a set of concepts that produce material explanations, no matter how counter-intuitive, no matter how mystifying to the uninitiated. Moreover, that materialism is an absolute, for we cannot allow a Divine Foot in the door."

Lewontin speaks of "we" referring to the secular scientists. They have a commitment to materialism despite the abundant evidence for God. What would happen if a Divine Foot *did* get in the door? The Divine Being would require accountability from the people He has created, and they don't like that.

The Moral Argument

Finally, we will address the moral argument for God. Scottish philosopher W. R. Sorley sums it up this way: "If morality is objective and absolute, God must exist. Morality is objective and absolute. Therefore, God must exist."

Without a moral law originating from a transcendent reference point higher than man and the material universe, there can be no way to determine what is good or evil. Man becomes the measure of all things. Good and evil become subjective, open to any opinion or interpretation. There is no

37

right or wrong, just personal opinion—a condition called moral relativism. Yet we all know there are objective moral absolutes. There are things we know are wrong, things like torturing and killing small babies for pleasure. Yet without a transcendent base for moral law we have no basis for saying anything is wrong.

Without God everything is subjective, yet we know inherently there is good and evil, as God has written the Law on our hearts (Roman 2). Some will say that popular opinion can determine what is right or wrong. Yet evil men have used popular opinion to justify doing evil things in the past, as in the case of slavery and the holocaust. If popular opinion is the standard, one must ask, on what basis can a person say these actions are wrong?

When Ravi Zacharias was asked why there is so much evil in the world, he responded: "When you say there's too much evil in this world you assume there's good. When you assume there's good, you assume there's such a thing as a moral law on the basis of which to differentiate between good and evil. But if you assume a moral law, you must posit a moral Law Giver, but that's Who you're trying to disprove and not prove. Because if there's no moral Law Giver, there's no moral law. If there's no moral law, there's no good. If there's no good, there's no evil. What is your question?" Zacharias makes a powerful argument for God using the moral argument.

The existence of evil is a problem for materialists. They can't answer why evil exists, and why there is not more or less evil in the world. The naturalists also have a problem defining evil. Biologist Richard Dawkins claims he rejects God because there is so much evil in the world. However, when asked to define evil, he states that there is no such thing as evil; he can't define it.

Pastor Jeffrey E. Ramey, MRE, writes, "Who decides what is right and wrong in the world? Who has the authority to define morality for all of creation? It is not the courts, congress, the media, public opinion, the 'politically correct' police, the 'tolerance' brigade or even the church. The only answer has been, is and always will be Jesus Christ. You can find His opinion on a great variety of subjects in His best seller...The Bible."

Christians know sin is the cause of evil, but we also know God is sovereign over sin. God did not design or create evil; we know it is a perversion of His creation. A new car is not made to rust but rust is a possible outcome for the car. God did not make us robots but gave us free choices. We were free to choose an alternative to God—that choice is known as "evil." We will have much more to say about evil and suffering in Chapter 7.

The evidence is clear: The origin of the universe points to the God of the Bible. The design of the universe, the laws of physics, and evidence of design in all of life point to an omniscient, omnipotent Creator, the God of the Bible. The presence of an objective moral law points to a Moral Law Giver, the God of the Bible.

Believing in the God of the Bible is the most reasonable and rational explanation for all of these observations. Any other conclusion would require a great deal more faith and even defy the laws of logic.

David Berlinski, an agnostic, in his book, <u>The Devil's</u> <u>Delusion</u>, poses these questions:

1) Has anyone provided a proof of God's inexistence? Not even close.
2) Has quantum cosmology explained the emergence of the universe or why it is here? Not even close.
3) Have the sciences explained why our universe seems to be fine-tuned to allow for the existence of life? Not even close.
4) Are physicists and biologists willing to believe in anything so long as it is not religious thought? Close enough.
5) Has rationalism in moral thought provided us with an understanding of what is good, what is right, and what is moral? Not close enough.
6) Has secularism in the terrible twentieth century been a force for good? Not even close to being close.
7) Is there a narrow and oppressive orthodoxy of thought and opinion within the sciences? Close enough.
8) Does anything in the sciences or in their philosophy justify the claim that religious belief is irrational? Not even in the ballpark.
9) Is scientific atheism a frivolous exercise in intellectual contempt? Dead on.

Chapter 3

Is the Bible the Word of God?

"We're not asking people to believe what the Bible says about God just 'because it says so.' No. We want people to believe the Bible because of the wealth of good evidence that has demonstrated the Bible to be trustworthy... hundreds of fulfilled prophecies...thousands of archaeological discoveries...numerous details in the Bible that have been corroborated by extra-biblical historical sources, and so on."

-Charlie H. Campbell

"The Bible is a collection of fantastic legends without scientific support."

-The Communist Dictionary

The Bible

The Bible is a remarkable collection of sixty-six separate books, written by forty authors from different backgrounds: kings, shepherds, prophets, fishermen, and a doctor. It was written in three different languages, on three different continents, over a period of 1,500 years. Yet the Bible proclaims a coherent message and a consistent theme. Each of its books is in harmony with all the others. No other religious manuscript comes close to the unity of the Bible and this unified message from such wide-ranging sources points to its inspiration from a higher source.

When one starts with the assumption there is a Creator God, then we can assume God has a purpose for creating the universe, the earth, and us. It would be logical to conclude that God would want to communicate that purpose to the world. One might ask, "How would an infinite God communicate His message to finite humans?" Recording a message in a book would be a logical means.

This Creator God had already given mankind the ability to understand spoken and written language. The Bible tells us God tried to speak directly to the Israelites, but the people asked to have His words written down instead. We believe God inspired Moses and the other authors of Scripture to write down His words and record His message in the Bible.

In his book, <u>Evidence That Demands a Verdict</u>, Christian apologist Josh McDowell notes that if God created man with a desire to know Him, we would expect His message to have some of the following unique properties:

1) It would be widely distributed so man could obtain it easily.
2) It would be preserved through time without corruption.
3) It would be completely accurate historically.
4) It would not be prone to scientific error or false beliefs held by the people of that time.
5) It would present true, unified answers to the difficult questions of life.

We will review each of these separately to see how the Bible meets these criteria.

Easily Obtained

Is God's message widely distributed and easily obtained? If the Creator God wished to communicate His message to the world, it would be no problem for Him to superintend the distribution of the message world-wide. The Bible not only meets this qualification but, in fact, is the only ancient religious manuscript that does.

The Bible has been published and translated into more languages than any other book throughout history. It has been a #1 bestseller ever since bestseller lists existed; in fact, it is no longer included on those lists because of this consistent record.

The Bible has been available throughout history despite efforts by many to destroy it. Voltaire was a French Enlightenment writer, historian, and philosopher who died in 1778. He vigorously attacked Christianity and the Bible and promised that within one hundred years of his time, Christianity and the Bible would be non-existent on the face of the earth and pass into the obscurity of history. Yet fifty years after his death, the Geneva Bible Society used his house in Switzerland, as well as his printing press, to produce thousands of Bibles. Today, in spite of many attempts to eliminate the Bible from history, it is found everywhere around the globe.

The Bible passes the first qualification with flying colors; no other ancient religious manuscript is so readily available today.

Preserved without Corruption

Has the content of the Bible been faithfully preserved over time? If God is sovereign, He would certainly be able to preserve His message throughout history. This is not to say that man or Satan wouldn't attempt to corrupt the

Scriptures. But God in His sovereignty would be able to preserve the original message in spite of these attempts. Other religions such as Islam and Mormonism claim that the Bible has been corrupted and their holy books are the corrected copy from God. However, without an original to prove the Bible has been corrupted, they do not have any evidence to back up those claims.

Instead we see from the evidence that while the original documents (called autographs) have not been preserved, God's message has. God did see to it that the early copies (called manuscripts) were preserved, and experts have used these copies to discern what the original autographs contained. Experts have been discovering older and older manuscripts that verify the Bible we have today is not corrupted.

Today there are more than 5,300 manuscripts or partial manuscripts of the New Testament. If we include the early translations of the Bible, the number rises to over 24,000. Writings outside of the Bible by early church theologians contain enough quotes from the New Testament that almost the entire New Testament could be reconstructed from them. They are consistent with what we have today.

Some suggest that there are discrepancies among the various copies. The New Testament contains roughly 20,000 lines of writing, of which only 40 lines are called into any kind of doubt. None of these lines substantially change any Biblical truth claims—most are minor differences such as variant spellings. The time gap between the original autograph and the earliest known copies is very small, in some cases as few as 35 years. We can be sure we have the message God wants us to have in the New Testament.

The Old Testament was preserved by the Hebrew people who meticulously copied the Scriptures, knowing they were God's own inspired words. The Jewish men who copied the Scriptures knew exactly how many letters were in every line and the number of lines in every book. This enabled them to check for errors by going back and counting each of the letters and lines, making sure no one had added, removed, or altered even one syllable. When the Dead Sea scrolls were discovered in the Qumran caves in 1948, the validity of the Old Testament Scriptures was greatly enhanced. Prior to their discovery, the earliest known manuscripts were from the tenth century A.D. The scrolls found in Qumran dated from 250 B.C. to A.D. 100. Copies of the Septuagint, the Greek version of the Old Testament, were translated around 250 B.C.

Comparisons of these ancient manuscripts to the later manuscripts show that the Scriptures have been accurately copied and amazingly preserved. The late Christian apologist and theologian Dr. Clark Pinnock says, "There exists no document from the ancient world witnessed by so excellent a set of textual and historical testimonies, and offering so superb an array of historical data on which the intelligent decision may be made. An honest [person] cannot dismiss a source of this kind. Skepticism regarding the historical credentials of Christianity is based upon an irrational bias." Thus the Bible meets this second qualification as well—it has been accurately preserved.

Historically Accurate

Do historical references in the Bible match up with other legitimate historical records? The only ancient religious manuscript that is set in a long span of history is the Bible—it was written over a period of 1,500 years. Just because the Bible is found to be historically accurate does not prove it is God's Word. However, it certainly would be called into question if it contained historical inconsistencies.

Archaeology has been a friend of the Bible. While not all historical claims of the Bible have been verified by archaeology, no archaeological discovery has in any way disproved the historical accuracy of the Bible. New discoveries are being made all the time that validate the Biblical historical accounts.

The evidence from archaeology verifying the Bible is so overwhelming that Christian archaeologist and Assyriologist Donald J. Wiseman, who studied the connections between archaeological discoveries and the Old Testament, concludes that more than 25,000 references to sites, customs, names, and events mentioned in the Bible have been found. Nelson Glueck, an American rabbi, academic, and archaeologist confirms this truth: "It may be stated categorically that no archaeological discovery has ever controverted a Biblical reference. Scores of archaeological findings have been made which confirm in clear outline or exact detail historical statements in the Bible. And, by the same token, proper evaluation of Biblical descriptions has often led to amazing discoveries." Archaeologist William F. Albright concurs: "Discovery after discovery has established the accuracy of innumerable details, and brought increased recognition of the value of the Bible as a source of history."

The events described in the New Testament took place in the first century, during the time of Christ and shortly thereafter. Several outside sources verify the people and events documented in the Bible –most notable is Flavius Josephus, a Jewish historian of that era. He refers to John the Baptist and his death at the hand of Herod. He also mentions James, the brother of Jesus, including his execution by the high priest Annas. The historian Josephus also wrote factually about the historical Jesus.

Other secular writers wrote of Jesus and his crucifixion; even the Jewish Talmud mentions Jesus' death occurring on the eve of Passover.

In A.D. 215, Julius Africanus, a North African Christian teacher, recorded the writing of a pagan historian by the name of Thallus. Thallus wrote in A.D. 52, only twenty years after the resurrection of Christ, that darkness totally covered the land at the time of the Passover that year. "As to [Jesus'] works severally, and His cures effected upon body and soul, and the mysteries of His doctrine, and the resurrection from the dead, these have been most authoritatively set forth by His disciples and apostles before us. On the whole world there pressed a most fearful darkness; and the rocks were rent by an earthquake, and many places in Judea and other districts were thrown down."

Early Christians were also described in contemporaneous non-Christian history. Pliny the Younger

(A.D. 61-113), in a letter to the Roman emperor Trajan, describes the lifestyles of early Christians: "They [Christians] were in the habit of meeting on a certain fixed day before it was light, when they sang in alternate verses a hymn to Christ, as to a god, and bound themselves by a solemn oath, not to any wicked deeds, but never to commit any fraud, theft or adultery, never to falsify their word, nor deny a trust when they should be called upon to deliver it up; after which it was their custom to separate, and then reassemble to partake of food—but food of an ordinary and innocent kind."

Cornelius Tacitus, known for his analysis and examination of historical documents, is among the most trusted of ancient historians. In "Annals" from A.D.116, he describes Emperor Nero's response to the great fire in Rome and Nero's claim that the Christians were to blame. "Consequently, to get rid of the report, Nero fastened the guilt and inflicted the most exquisite tortures on a class hated for their abominations, called Christians by the populace. Christus, from whom the name had its origin, suffered the extreme penalty during the reign of Tiberius at the hands of one of our procurators, Pontius Pilatus, and a most mischievous superstition, thus checked for the moment, again broke out not only in Judea, the first source of the evil, but even in Rome, where all things hideous and shameful from every part of the world find their centre and become popular."

In contrast, the Book of Mormon, written in 1830, refers to historical events, but it does not stand up under the historical accuracy test. It includes historical accounts that were believed to be true at the time but have since been proved wrong. It describes the lost tribes of Israel coming to America, but DNA tests have disproved this. It reports that the Americas were covered with the "mound builders," but archaeologists have concluded that these were a localized tribe and did not live across the country. The mound builder theory was popular in America in Joseph Smith's time, and the book of Mormon is based on those theories of men, not inspired from God. The early Mormons referred to the mound builder theories to substantiate the Book of Mormon as being historically accurate, but they seek to discount them today. This would certainly cause one to question the supernatural origins of the Book of Mormon. The National Geographic Society confirms this problem: "Archaeologists and other scholars have long probed the hemisphere's past, and the Society does not know of anything found so far that has substantiated the Book of Mormon."

The Bible stands alone in meeting this qualification of historical accuracy. This truth is validated by archaeologist John Elder (quoting from Don Stewart's The Ten Wonders of the Bible): "It is not too much to say that it was the rise of the science of archeology that broke the deadlock between historians and the orthodox Christian. Little by little, one city after another, one civilization after another, one culture after another, whose memories were enshrined only in the Bible, were restored to their proper place in ancient history by the studies of archeologists....The over-all result is indisputable. Forgotten cities have been found, the handiwork of vanished peoples has reappeared, contemporary records of Biblical events have been unearthed and the uniqueness of Biblical revelation has been emphasized by contrast and comparison to the newly understood religions of ancient peoples. Nowhere has archaeological discovery refuted the Bible as history."

Scientific Accuracy

The fourth qualification for authenticity noted above considers whether the Bible can be considered scientifically accurate.

Archaeology has verified historical events, places, and people, as we saw in the last section. Some of the truth claims in the wisdom books have been verified and modern science validates many of the cleansing and medical treatments prescribed in the ceremonial laws. Of course, since the Bible is an ageless, timeless document, it does not use the scientific terms we use today.

True scientific investigation is careful to examine all evidence without a prior assumption or model, and then use deductive reasoning to reach the best explanation. When "science" has a prior agenda, it will selectively use facts not representative of the full body of evidence and reach a conclusion that does not match the preponderance of evidence.

So-called "scientific discoveries" have been put forward that purport to contradict the Bible. This includes Darwinian evolution, which we will see is in no way a proven fact. When theologians accept this pseudo-science and change their interpretation of the Bible, for example to deny the literal historic accuracy of the first eleven chapters of Genesis, we are on a slippery slope of further compromise that denies the power and glory of God as revealed in His creation.

In Chapter 2, we saw that the Bible speaks of creating the universe out of nothing, and noted how this is consistent with recent scientific conclusions. In one of his sermons, Christian pastor John MacArthur explained how the first verse of the Bible is scientifically validated. "A well-known scientist, a very decorated scientist named Herbert Spencer died in 1903. In his scientific career he had become noted for one great discovery, it was a categorical contribution that he made. He discovered that all reality, all reality, all that exists in the universe can be contained in five categories: time, force, action, space and matter. Herbert Spencer said everything that exists, exists in one of those categories: time, force, action, space and matter. Nothing exists outside of those categories. That was a very astute discovery and didn't come until the nineteenth century. Now think about that. Spencer even listed them in that order: time, force, action, space and matter. That is a logical sequence. And then with that in your mind, listen to Genesis 1:1. 'In the beginning [that's time], God [that's force] created [that's action] the heavens [that's space] and the earth [that's matter].' In the first verse of the Bible God said plainly what man didn't catalog until the nineteenth century. Everything that could be said about everything that exists is said in that first verse."

Genesis 1:6-7 accurately describes the water inside the earth: "Then God said, 'Let there be an expanse in the midst of the waters, and let it separate the waters from the waters.' God made the expanse, and separated the waters which were below the expanse from the waters which were above the expanse; and it was so." Based on a geological discovery, a recent article in <u>Nature</u> (March 2014) concludes, "There could be an ocean's worth of water more than 300 miles under the Earth's surface that equals the known water content across the entire planet." No other worldview, certainly not evolution, would have predicted this.

In Isaiah 40:22, the Bible describes the earth as a circle or sphere, mentioning that God sits "above the circle of the earth." Many pagan beliefs at the time held to a flat earth; the Bible never has. The book of Job (the most ancient of Biblical books) in chapter 26 verse 7 says: "He stretches out the northern skies over empty space; He hangs the earth on nothing." This confirms the earth is in space hanging on nothing—a concept not found in any of the ancient myths. For example, the Hindu Vedas taught that the earth is set atop the backs of elephants which are standing on four giant sea-turtles swimming through a milky sea.

In Psalm 102:26, David speaks of the universe "wearing out like a garment," consistent with the second law of thermodynamics (the law of entropy). The Bible tells us on the seventh day God had finished working and rested. Genesis 1:31: "And God saw all that He had made and it was very good." God was done creating, which includes the creation of any new energy. This fact is consistent with the first law of thermodynamics, and demonstrates that energy must be created by a supernatural force.

Jeremiah 33:22 says the stars are countless—as many as the grains of sand on the seashore. That is a very close description and it was a concept unthinkable at the time as only a few thousand stars are visible from earth.

The Bible describes the water cycle in Ecclesiastes 1:7: "All the rivers run into the sea, yet the sea is not full; to the place from which the rivers come, there they return again." Job 38:16 refers to "the springs of the sea." Only recently have springs on the bottom of the sea been discovered. Psalm 8:8 speaks of the paths of the sea; consistent with this passage, scientists have found definite ocean currents that ships now use to their advantage. Ecclesiastes 1:6 describes the wind blowing in circular paths; this was not known at the time, but today we know it to be true.

Leviticus 17:11 tells us, "...the life of the flesh is in the blood." We know today that blood is fundamental to the function of every cell in every part of our bodies. This wasn't always known. At one time it was believed that blood-letting was a legitimate medical cure for ills, but today we know blood is a vital fluid.

Good hygiene practices, such as washing thoroughly after touching a corpse or someone's blood, are demanded by Leviticus 15:10-12. This was first practiced within the medical community about 150 years ago. Before that time medical doctors did not wash between surgeries or after touching a corpse, which resulted in the spread of infectious diseases. The fantastic results of this "discovery" have saved an untold number of lives.

Deuteronomy 23:12-13 instructs, "Designate a place outside the camp where you can go to relieve yourself. As part of your equipment have something to dig with, and when you relieve yourself, dig a hole and cover up your excrement." This seems rather obvious in today's world. However, many cultures in the past did not follow this advice and, as a result, diseases spread readily.

Charlie Campbell, director of the Always Be Ready Apologetics Ministry, makes this point: "One of the things that sets the Bible apart from all other ancient religious writings is its scientific accuracy. Without exception, every other ancient religious writing contains certain scientific errors. For example, Muhammad taught in the Qur'an that the sun descends down into a muddy spring. The Hindu Vedas state that the Earth is flat and triangular and that earthquakes are caused by elephants shaking themselves under it. You'll never read absurd statements like those in the Bible."

The Bible has amazingly passed this science-based test. No other religious manuscript comes close.

Answers Difficult Questions

The final qualification for authenticity relates to how the Bible addresses the big, difficult questions of life. In fact, the Bible answers the most important question, where did we come from? There are two possible explanations for our origin: "time plus chance" or a supernatural creation. We presented the evidence for the Creator God in the previous chapter.

Another difficult question is how to discern the meaning of life…in other words, what gives life purpose? We want our lives to have significance. Recent findings from

Dartmouth Medical School suggest that children are biologically "hardwired" for enduring attachments to other people and for moral and spiritual meaning.

The God of the Bible fulfills this enduring attachment void; He gives us true moral and spiritual meaning eternally. If we were here as the result of an accident of time plus chance, then once we have passed into history, what difference would it make if we had acted like Jesus or like Hitler? The message of the Bible is that our lives *do* have meaning, that there is purpose for us being here, and the consequences of the way we live now are eternal. Our purpose is to love God and glorify Him, and then to love our fellow humans. This is the foundation for living our lives.

We all have experienced joy from loving and helping others. But without God there is no philosophical or theological reason for doing so. Without God, whether a person helps or hurts someone makes no difference in the long run. The Bible shows that suffering in this world has meaning and purpose. As Ravi Zacharias says: "The Biblical world-view is the only one that accepts the reality of evil and suffering while giving both the cause and the purpose, while offering God-given strength and sustenance in the midst of it." We will explore suffering and evil in depth in Chapter 7.

Having hope is very important. We humans seem to want to have hope for the future. Christianity gives us true hope, as Paul tells us in 1 Corinthians 2:9, "Eye has not seen, nor ear heard, nor has it entered into the heart of man the things which God has prepared for those who love Him." Heaven is a place that is beautiful beyond anything we have seen, heard, or can imagine. This is our hope. If we have trusted Christ as our Savior, we have this hope. And every day we live with the reality of Romans 15:13: "May the God of hope fill you with all joy and peace as you trust in Him, so that you may overflow with hope by the power of the Holy Spirit." The purpose, the meaning, the security, and the hope we have as the result of Christ's gift of salvation to us are for now and for all eternity.

Hinduism, Jainism, Buddhism, and Sikhism offer the possibility of a Nirvana-type state in the future. It is seen as a type of liberation (moksha) from the world into nothingness, an eternal connection with the impersonal force of the universe. That is not a very happy future for those who understand the religion. Islam describes heaven as a very sensual place. I believe Mohammad got this idea from Zoroastrianism. It is not a comforting promise for women, but it is what one would expect from the imagination of an immoral man. These religions believe followers can achieve heaven through their good works. However, none can state how many good works are sufficient. They offer no sure hope.

The final fundamental area of questions for which we seek answers: "What is mankind's problem? What is the solution?" The Bible describes the heart of man as being depraved—selfish and in rebellion against God, but it is redeemable! God offers this redemption to us freely by the sacrifice of His own Son to pay the debt we never could. No other worldview offers this hope of salvation as a free offer from a gracious and loving God. Muslims believe man is born fundamentally good. Modern Jews believe man is born neutral, like a blank slate.

British journalist Malcolm Muggeridge states the problem very well: "The depravity of man is at once the most empirically verifiable reality but at the same time the most intellectually resisted fact." The problem with man is sin. Because sinful mankind can do nothing to attain the standards of a perfect God, he needs a Savior. Jesus' sacrifice is the solution and God's Word is our guide.

Changing Lives

The Bible is further validated as God's word when peoples' lives are changed for the better when they follow its directions. The Bible has changed communities, prisons, and nations for the better. Toronto, Canada is a good example. William Howland, a Christian man, was elected mayor of Toronto in 1885 and fought for the poor, against corruption in city hall, and against vice in the community. Mayor Howland helped clean up Toronto morally and physically during a dark time in its history. He signaled his arrival in the mayor's office by installing a twelve-foot banner on the wall, reading, "Except the Lord Build the City, the Watchman Wakes but in Vain." Despite fierce opposition, Howland succeeded in transforming the city, so much so that Toronto was known as "Toronto the Good" long after he left office. We have seen amazing things throughout history when the people of a nation put their trust in God and follow His word. This has been true in the past of England, Holland, and the United States.

Angola prison in Louisiana is another example. This was once known as the bloodiest prison in America. It is home to some 5,000 murderers, rapists, and other violent criminals. A new warden came in and promised to make changes through Biblical "moral rehabilitation" and the introduction of voluntary, faith-based programs. A Bible college was started on the prison grounds and it produces about 150 preachers each year, many of whom are sent to prisons around the state. After 18 years, Angola is probably the safest prison in America today; the change defies human explanation. The average recidivism (repeat offender) rate in secular prisons is 77%, compared to just 8% of prisoners who go through voluntary, faith-based Christian programs while in prison.

Another example comes from Dr. Harry Ironside, who was presenting the gospel in the San Francisco area early in his ministry when one day he was challenged by an atheist who claimed atheism has done more for the world than Christianity. He further challenged Dr. Ironside to a debate: "Atheism versus Christianity." "You Christians never want to debate based on facts, just your feelings," he challenged. "This will be about facts. Are you interested?"

Dr. Ironside accepted, but added a condition. The atheist was to bring one man and one woman who had struggled for years to leave behind a life down and out in the gutter and were only able to change for the better because of atheism. Dr. Ironside promised to bring 100 men and 100 women who had lived a depraved lifestyle and whose lives were miraculously changed by the saving power of Jesus Christ. "Real people, real lives, real change – just the facts."

The atheist waved his hand at Dr. Ironside and walked away. There was no debate.

The Bible gives answers to fundamental life questions related to meaning, hope, man's problem, and God's solution in the Lord Jesus Christ. Christianity is the only religion that puts forward a guarantee of salvation freely offered to all through the Lord Jesus Christ, Who infuses our lives with hope and meaning. The Bible passes this qualification as no other religious manuscript can.

Evolution does not have the answers to these questions, as atheist William B. Provine, Professor of Biological Science at Cornell University, admits (Origins Research 16(1), pp. 9 and 123): "Let me summarize my views on what modern evolutionary biology tells us loud and clear....There are no gods, no purposes, and no goal-directed forces of any kind. There is no life after death. When I die, I am absolutely certain that I am going to be dead. That's the end for me. There is no ultimate foundation for ethics, no ultimate meaning to life, and no free will for humans either."

Fulfilled Prophecy

Prophecy fulfillment is another important way to verify the Bible is the word of God. The Bible tells us to discern if a prophetic message is truly coming from God by watching to see if it is fulfilled. Deuteronomy 18:20-22 states, "But the prophet who shall speak a word presumptuously in My name which I have not commanded him to speak, or which he shall speak in the name of other gods, that prophet shall die. And you may say in your heart,

'How shall we know the word which the LORD has not spoken?' When a prophet speaks in the name of the LORD, if the thing does not come about or come true, that is the thing the LORD has not spoken. The prophet has spoken it presumptuously; you shall not be afraid of him."

In 2 Peter 1:21 the apostle Peter states, "No prophecy was ever made by an act of human will, but men moved by the Holy Spirit spoke from God." No other religious texts give specific, detailed prophecies as the Bible does. Let's examine a few prophecies to demonstrate their accuracy.

The Bible contains more than 2,000 prophesies that have been fulfilled, many in very specific detail, including predictions of the rise and fall of empires, nations, cities, and individuals. All of them have proved entirely accurate. This includes many predictions about Israel—some of which have been fulfilled in the past and others that will be in the future.

Charlie H. Campbell validates this truth, "No other book in the world is able to substantiate its claims with this kind of supernatural ability to rightly foretell human events. There are no fulfilled prophecies in the Quran, the Hindu Vedas, the Book of Mormon, or any other sacred religious writings. Not one. Fulfilled prophecy is something that sets the Bible apart from every other religious book."

The promise of the coming of the Jewish Messiah is the focus of the Old Testament. There are more than 300 separate prophecies about the Messiah. Many are so specific that they predict the city of Jesus' birth (Bethlehem) (Micah

5:2), His Divine nature (Isaiah 7:14), His works of healing and miracles (Isaiah 35:5-6), His betrayal for thirty pieces of silver (Zechariah 11:12-13), His suffering (Isaiah 53), His style of execution (Psalm 22), and His resurrection (Psalm 16:10, Acts 13:35), along with many other fulfilled prophecies. These were written anywhere from 400 to 1,000 years before Jesus' birth, yet they describe His life with the accuracy of an eyewitness.

The odds against any living person fulfilling even a few of these predictions are so astronomical it is considered impossible. Mathematician Peter W. Stoner and theologian Robert C. Newman collaborated on a book entitled Science Speaks. Based on the science of probability, the book and its findings were verified by the American Scientific Affiliation. The authors calculated the odds of any one man in all of history fulfilling even eight of the 60 major prophecies (and 270 ramifications) fulfilled by the life of Christ. The probability that Jesus of Nazareth could have fulfilled even eight such prophecies would be only 1 in 10 to the 17th power (1 in 100,000,000,000,000,000). Stoner points out that many silver dollars would be enough to cover the surface of the entire state of Texas to a depth of two feet. The odds for all the prophecies being fulfilled in one person would be the same as a blindfolded man, heading out of Dallas by foot in any direction, being able on his very first attempt to pick up one specifically marked silver dollar out of 100,000,000,000,000,000. Theoretically it is possible, but in reality it just isn't going to happen. What chance would the prophets have of writing these eight prophecies hundreds of year before and having them all fulfilled in the life of any one man if they had written them without God's inspiration? The odds are staggeringly small.

Evidence for the Resurrection

Jesus himself predicted His death and resurrection. Jesus validated who He was through the miracles He performed while on earth, but He validated everything He said and did through His resurrection from the grave. By His resurrection from the grave, He validated that His work of redemption was completed on the cross and He demonstrated He had won the victory over death. This includes His statement that the Scriptures are God's words and God's Word is true. If He truly rose from the dead, as He said He would, then we can trust everything else He said and did. This means it is very important that we know the evidence for the resurrection.

What is the evidence? Antony Flew was a devout defender of atheism. He eventually became a theist after being shown repeatedly the evidence for Christ's resurrection while debating Christian scholars. After several debates, Flew concluded that, "The evidence for the resurrection is better than for claimed miracles in any other religion. It's outstandingly different in quality and quantity." Since His resurrection validates what Christ did on the cross for us as well as everything He said and did, we can base our faith on objective reality. Ours can be a reasonable faith based on evidence. Let's look at the evidence.

First is the empty tomb. Jesus' human body was placed in a tomb protected by soldiers. The Bible tells us local women were the first to find the grave empty. If the story were made up, women would not have been witnesses, since in that historical era, a woman's testimony was not considered as credible as a man's. Jesus was also buried in strips of burial clothes like a mummy—these were found as an empty shell with no body in them, also evidence of the resurrection. The story given out at the time to explain the disappearance was that the disciples stole the body while the soldiers guarding the grave slept. Could the disciples have stolen His body? The tomb was very well guarded by Roman soldiers and the disciples at the time were hiding behind locked doors in fear of those soldiers. (If the guards were asleep how could they claim to know who stole the body?) Further, if the disciples had stolen the body, why would they leave the burial cloths behind? Finally, if the Jewish leaders had been able to produce the body, as they surely strove to do, the Christian movement would have abruptly ended.

The appearance of the resurrected Christ to his followers explains how they went from scared, defeated individuals to bold evangelists willing to die for the gospel. They were even willing to be tortured and killed for their beliefs.

People will die for a lie if they think it is true, but they will not die for what they know to be a lie. The disciples claimed to be eyewitnesses and had opportunities to save their own lives by refuting their story, but they refused. Their willingness to die for their beliefs is an indication that they knew it was the truth.

One might ask what their motive was. Was it fame and fortune? No, historical records show they were hated and persecuted. Yet they were transformed from frightened men to bold witnesses by their witness of the resurrection. They led a massive revival that resulted in thousands coming to Christ, as many as 3,000 in one day. The rapid expansion of the church in the face of persecution is also evidence of the resurrection.

In 1 Corinthians 15:14,17 Paul says our faith is in vain if Christ is not resurrected. He lists several people who were eyewitnesses, including 500 at one time (1 Corinthians 15:6), and the readers could talk to them directly since most were still alive at the time of his writing. I believe the evidence for the resurrection passes the credibility test in every way.

Jesus' Claim to be Deity

Jesus is the unique Person of all of History. He was eternally God in heaven, yet He humbled Himself to be born of a virgin as a perfect man. He remained undiminished deity and perfect true humanity in one Person—the only Being qualified to redeem us from the penalty of our sin and willing to make that tremendous sacrifice while we were still His enemies. He claimed to have existed from the beginning, been with God, and to be God and Creator. (John 1:1-3) He performed numerous unique miracles witnessed by many people while He was on the earth, validating His Divine origin. He claimed that only He was the Way, the Truth, and the Life (John 14:6) and that no one can come to God (the Father) except through Him. As we have seen, His resurrection verifies the complete effectiveness of His sacrifice for our salvation. Jesus was unique in claiming to be God and His impact on the world is undeniable. No other religion claims to have a God Who eternally saves sinners and offers that salvation freely to anyone who will believe in Him.

God of the Bible is one God but in three persons. If God was only one, He could not love without an object for that love. Being three persons God can love, because in the community of the Trinity there is love for each other from all eternity. Being absolutely perfect, God cannot tolerate associating with sin. Sinning against an infinite God requires infinite payment for God's justice to be satisfied. But the one paying would not only have to be infinite but also truly human. Jesus has always been infinite, and He chose to become truly human. He was the only One who could pay the price and He paid it for all. We could try to pay the price, but as finite beings we could never pay it. All we can do is trust in Him as our Savior and Redeemer.

The Story of the Bible

The story of the Bible in one word is *redemption*. The first two chapters describe the initial paradise created by God. This is followed by 1,185 chapters of "messy sinfulness" with the promise of redemption for those who believed in that promise prior to the cross and in the fulfilled work for those who believed after the cross. In the last two chapters of the final book of the Bible, Revelation, we see paradise regained! That was made possible by the redeeming work of Jesus Christ alone.

The Old Testament looks forward with hope for the seed of the woman who would crush the head of the serpent and bruise His heel as promised in Genesis 3:15. Jesus was that One—the cross is the central story of the Bible and of all history. The Bible is God's message to us and it is God's revelation of Himself to us...how He loves us, how He provided us a way back to Him, how He wants us to live, and how He wants to have a personal relationship with each person He has created.

Conclusion

Let's conclude this chapter with a testimonial from R.A. Torrey (1856–1928), an American evangelist, pastor, educator, and writer. "I was brought up to believe that the Bible was the Word of God. In early life I accepted it as such upon the authority of my parents, and never gave the question any serious thought. But later in life my faith in the Bible was utterly shattered through the influence of the writings of a very celebrated, scholarly and brilliant skeptic. I found myself face to face with the question: Why do you believe the Bible is the Word of God? I had no satisfactory answer. I determined to go to the bottom of this question. If satisfactory proof could not be found that the Bible was God's Word I would give the whole thing up, cost what it might. If satisfactory proof could be found that the Bible was God's Word I would take my stand upon it, cost what it might. I doubtless had many friends who could have answered the question satisfactorily, but I was unwilling to confide to them the struggle that was going on in my own heart; so I sought help from God and from books, and after much painful study and thought came out of the darkness of skepticism into the broad daylight of faith and certainty that the Bible from beginning to end is God's Word."

I hope, based on the evidence presented in this chapter and the rest of this book, you come to the same conclusion.

Chapter Four

Two Views of the Fossil Record: Catastrophism or Uniformitarianism

"The one who states his case first seems right, until the other comes and examines him."

-Proverbs 18:17

"A fair result can be obtained only by fully stating and balancing the facts and arguments on both sides of each question."

-Charles Darwin, On the Origin of Species, 1859

Hearing Both Sides

Imagine you are arrested and charged with a crime, but are not allowed to present evidence in your defense. You might be granted a "show trial," but you cannot cross examine witnesses or give your side of the story. Surely, an innocent person would be punished for crimes he or she had never committed. I think we can all agree this would not be right or just.

Unfortunately, this is happening in secular science today. In the creation/evolution debate, the creation view is not being heard. Only one side of the story is told in academia; creationists are not allowed to question the theory of evolution. The idea of evolution has not been fairly debated in institutions of higher learning in more than 50 years.

In universities, students are told evolution is a settled scientific fact and professors often compare creationists to believers in a flat earth—in fact Darwin did this. They are saying, indirectly, that creationism is anti-science. That is not intellectually honest and the comparisons are not valid.

After all, we can verify the earth is spherical by sending up space probes or watching a ship disappear over the horizon. Science has proven the earth's shape. But we cannot send a time machine back into the past to observe how geological changes occurred over time. Secular science has concluded that the fossil record is evidence for long periods of time. But this is far from proven, as we will see.

This chapter will review the case for "long ages"—the assumption that the earth is billions of years old, also known as "uniformitarianism." In contrast, "catastrophism" is the traditional Biblical explanation for the evidence left behind from a global flood. We will examine the fossil record and other geological formations, and determine if an honest examination of this evidence is more consistent with catastrophism or uniformitarianism. Then, in Chapter 5, we will look at Darwinian Evolution.

The Catastrophic vs. the Uniformitarian Model

The catastrophism model, by definition, maintains that Earth has been changed in the past by a sudden, short-lived, violent event planet-wide in scope. This model is in contrast to uniformitarianism (sometimes known as gradualism), which holds that slow incremental changes, such as erosion and wind, are the only factors necessary to explain all of Earth's geological features. Uniformitarianism, by definition, denies the possibility that there were any worldwide catastrophes in the past, especially a world-wide flood as described in the Bible.

Biblical Evidence for the Flood

Let us investigate the evidence for the worldwide catastrophic flood. Our first eyewitness to interview is the Bible.

The book of Genesis is an historical narrative, an eyewitness account, inspired by God and written by Moses. According to Genesis 7:20, "The waters rose and covered the mountains to a depth of more than fifteen cubits [22 feet]." Jesus corroborated the flood narrative in Luke 17:27: "Noah went into the ark and the flood came and killed them all." And again in Matthew 24:38-39: "And knew not until the flood came, and took them all away; so shall also the coming of the Son of man be." Jesus said *all* were killed or taken away in a worldwide flood. It is clear He is speaking of a worldwide catastrophic event, comparing it to His final judgment of all people.

These passages clearly describe a global flood. The waters are said to have remained for over a year. The stated reason for the flood was God's judgment on man, and its purpose was to destroy all humans on the earth except for Noah and his family. When it was over, God promised to never flood the world again, and He gave the rainbow as the sign of His promise. God would be going back on His word if this had been a localized flood, since many of these have occurred throughout history.

71

The Hebrew word used for the Genesis flood is
mabul. It is used several times in passages that describe the
flood in Genesis 6-9, and is not used anywhere else in the
Bible to describe any other flood event. It is a unique word
used only for this catastrophic occurrence. There are eight
other Hebrew words used to describe local floods, but none of
them are used in the context of the Genesis flood.

Psalm 104:6-9 describes the flood (from the Message
translation): "You blanketed earth with ocean, covered the
mountains with deep waters; Then you roared and the water
ran away, your thunder crash put it to flight. Mountains
pushed up, valleys spread out in the places you assigned
them. You set boundaries between earth and sea; never
again will earth be flooded." This describes a worldwide
catastrophic flood and, very significantly, mountains
forming rapidly immediately afterwards.

2 Peter 3:3-7 says, "Above all, you must understand
that in the last days scoffers will come, scoffing and
following their own evil desires. They will say, 'Where is this
'coming' he promised? Ever since our ancestors died,
everything goes on as it has since the beginning of creation
[uniformitarianism].' But they deliberately forget that long
ago by God's word the heavens came into being and the
earth was formed out of water and by water. By these
waters also the world of that time was deluged and
destroyed. By the same word the present heavens and earth
are reserved for fire, being kept for the Day of Judgment and
destruction of the ungodly."

Peter reiterates that there was a worldwide flood. He
warns of scoffers who will come in the last days and

deliberately forget about the flood, and will instead accept uniformitarianism. He compares the destruction of all mankind in the flood to the final judgment, when the ungodly will all be judged by fire.

There are many ancient flood legends and since they claim to be from witnesses they must be heard. Many cultures around the world have passed down a flood legend narrative through the generations. Most are remarkably similar to the Biblical flood story.

Dr. John Morris and the Institute for Creation Research (ICR.org) have collected more than 300 flood legends from around the world. He grouped the truth claims common in these legends and compiled the percentage of the legends making each truth claim. Is there a favored family? 88%. Are they forewarned? 66%. Is the flood due to the wickedness of man? 66%. Is the catastrophe only a flood? 95%. Was the flood global? 95%. Is survival due to a boat? 70%. Are animals also saved? 67%. Do animals play any part? 73%. Do survivors land on a mountain? 57%.

Clearly, the majority of the legends are consistent with the idea of a catastrophic global flood and the details of the Biblical flood. Ancient civilizations, separated by geography and language, would not likely have narratives so similar if there had not been an actual flood event which they had heard about through the generations.

Lyell, the Father of Modern Geology and Uniformitarianism

One might ask, "How did scientists ever come to believe that the fossil record represents long ages?" As we saw in 2 Peter 3:3, the apostle Peter predicted that in the last days, scoffers would emerge and deliberately dismiss the flood idea.

The first notable geologist to dismiss the catastrophic flood model and conclude the fossil record represented long time periods was James Hutton (1726-1797). He stated, "The past history of our globe must be explained by what can be seen to be happening now." Hutton did not have a major influence on geology in his time, but Charles Lyell (1797-1875), a lawyer and amateur geologist, noted Hutton's ideas and published three volumes in the 1830s titled, Principles of Geology: Being an Attempt to Explain the Former Changes of the Earth's Surface by Reference to Causes Now in Operation.

Lyell coined the term and popularized the concept of "uniformitarianism." Uniformitarianism, the idea that the earth was shaped in the past by the same processes still in operation today, is summed up by the phrase: "The present is the key to the past."

Lyell's book did not attempt to build the case for uniformitarianism, but rather attacked the belief in the flood of Genesis, in the same way a defense attorney attacks the case of the prosecution without building an alternate scenario. His primary argument was there are no global catastrophic activities occurring now, so why should we think there were any in the past? He pointed out that the laws of physics don't change, so why would we suggest things have changed on the earth?

A paradigm is a framework containing the basic assumptions, ways of thinking, and methodology that are commonly accepted by members of a community, such as a cognitive framework shared by members of any scientific discipline. In this case, Lyell started a major paradigm shift in science. Lyell hated the Bible and hated that science validated the Bible. He wanted to use science to disprove the Bible...all without mentioning the Bible. He built on John Hutton's idea that the fossil record not only wasn't evidence of the flood, but also represented long periods, much longer than the Biblical narrative allowed.

The Church of England quickly accepted uniformitarianism. Church leaders embraced his idea and in 1831 Lyell was appointed to the position of Professor of Geology at the new King's College in London. The major church denominations ran all the universities and Lyell's ideas quickly spread through the university systems.

These institutions replaced their old geology books with Lyell's books. Geologists had not accepted the uniformitarian model, but in teaching students only the uniformitarian idea and not any of the evidence for the Biblical view, they were able to bring about a very rapid paradigm shift. We can only speculate why church leaders of the major liberal denominations accepted the way Lyell used "science" to disprove the Bible, but history tells us they were known for immoral lifestyles at the time.

Lyell's agenda against the Bible is apparent in letters written to a friend, English geologist George P. Scrope. On June 14, 1830, Lyell wrote, "I am sure you may get into QR (Quarterly Review) what will free the science from Moses, for if treated seriously the (church) party are ready for it....I conceived the idea five or six years ago that if ever the Mosaic geology could be set down without giving offence, it would be in an historical sketch, and you must extract mine, in order to say as little as possible yourself."

As a lawyer, Lyell was not involved in scientific investigation, but he used his influence in a political power game to ensure his uniformitarian ideas would be accepted by the church. He knew the ideas clearly contradicted the plain reading of Scripture as he sought to disprove the flood and prove the world was much older than the Bible indicates.

Lyell went out of his way in this regard on a later trip to the Niagara Falls. Local scientists had measured the rate of erosion of the river and knew how much it had eroded in the past. They estimated there had been roughly 4,400 years of erosion—a number consistent with the Biblical timing of the flood. Lyell did his own calculations and published his findings, saying that the local scientists were all wrong and the evidence pointed to a much older date. His paper carried significant weight and was accepted as fact. However, later investigation revealed that he ignored the evidence, used bad science, and made up numbers to build his case.

Lyell's secretive scheming to deliberately put aside the evidence of the flood not only deceived the church leaders, but it also sent geology down the wrong path.

Warren Allmon, Ph.D., Professor of Paleontology in the Department of Earth and Atmospheric Sciences at

Cornell University points this out: "As is now increasingly acknowledged, however, Lyell sold geology some snake oil. He convinced geologists that because physical laws are constant...it necessarily follows that all past processes acted at their present rates...this extreme gradualism led to numerous unfortunate consequences, including the rejection of sudden catastrophic events in the face of positive evidence for them for no reason other than that they were not gradual." (Allmon, Science 262, October 1993, p. 122)

Derek Ager, Professor Emeritus of Geology at the University College of Swansea and former President of the British Geological Association, states, "...we have allowed ourselves to be brain-washed into avoiding any interpretation of the past that involves extreme and what might be termed 'catastrophic' processes." (The Nature of the Stratigraphic Record, 1993, p. 70)

In the same piece, he provides more insights into this issue: "Uniformitarianism triumphed...Catastrophism became a joke....But I would like to suggest that, in the first half of the last century, the catastrophists were better geologists than the uniformitarians." (pp. 67-68)

Steven J. Gould, an evolutionist and former paleontologist for the Chicago Museum of Natural History, states, "To many scientists (of the 19th Century) natural cataclysm seemed as threatening as the reign of terror....Contrary to popular myths, Darwin and Lyell were not the heroes of true science, defending objectivity.... Catastrophists were as committed to science as any gradualist, in fact, they adopted the more objective view."

(Evolution's Rapid Pace, Natural History, 86, No.5, April-May 1977, pp. 12-16)

Darwin noted in his journals: "Lyell is most firmly convinced he has shaken the faith in the Deluge [Noah's Flood] far more efficiently by never having said a word against the Bible than if he had acted otherwise....I have lately read Morely's Life of Voltaire, and he insists strongly that direct attacks on Christianity (even when written with the wonderful force and vigor of Voltaire) produce little permanent effect; real good seems only to follow the slow and silent side attacks." (Gertrude Himmelfarb, Darwin and the Darwinian Revolution, 1967, p. 387)

Evidence for the Flood

Common experiences can provide relevant information to this investigation. For example, anyone who has spent time at the beach has observed that fish and other creatures are found dead there all the time. But their carcasses don't lie around for thousands of years. In fact, they are eaten up or decay rather rapidly...within a few days in most cases. Experiments with recently dead fish reveal that, in water, their skeletons will fall apart and disintegrate in less than one week.

Finding fish still intact in the fossil record is strong evidence for rapid burial. As a homicide detective, I have seen that human corpses do not lay around for thousands of years either. When the bodies are left exposed to wild animals and other natural elements, there is very little left after a few months. If a body is buried at the time of death, it will be preserved much longer. Thus it is more logical that rapid burial, shortly after death, is a more likely explanation for the intact fish found in the fossil record.

In other words, the principle of experiential relevance applied to the fossil record tells us that dead bodies do not remain intact for long ages while they become hardened into fossils. The discovery of many intact fish skeletons is much more consistent with a catastrophic flood event, quickly preserving the creatures found in the fossil record.

What else does the evidence left behind tell us about what happened in the past? First we know that the earth's surface area is 70% covered with water. It is estimated that if the land and the sea floor were all at the same elevation, this amount of water would be a mile and a half deep over the surface. We also know that 75% of the surface area of all the continents in the world is covered with sedimentary rock.

Sedimentary rocks are formed by dirt, sand, and rock that have been eroded by fast moving water and carried to another location. The water lays down sediment at the new location, forming layered sedimentary rocks. All fossils recorded are found in sedimentary rock. On the surface of the continents, sedimentary rock varies in depth, averaging approximately one mile in thickness, with some areas greater than ten miles thick. How did the sedimentary rock and the fossils get there? How long did it take? Let us look at the evidence.

Of the fossils found in sedimentary rock, 95% are marine invertebrates (an animal lacking a backbone), mainly shellfish and clams. Of the remaining 5%, 95% are algae and plant fossils and 95% of the remaining 0.25% are other invertebrates, including insects. The remaining 0.0125% includes all vertebrates (animals with a backbone or spinal column), mostly fish. Very few of the fossils discovered are land vertebrates, and 95% of the few land vertebrates found consist of a single bone or partial bone (The Young Earth, Morris, J.D., 1994).

This evidence is consistent with a worldwide flood as the vast majority of creatures and plants in the fossil record come from the sea and very few from land.

The fossil record as presented in high school or college textbooks typically shows layering of different fossilized creatures representing long time periods. They assume equal quantities of all different types of animals are found as fossils. The only place one will find a fossil record like that is in the textbooks themselves. In the real world, sea creatures are found in all layers, and the layers are not in the same order in most locations.

As mentioned, land creatures found in the fossil record are typically found in parts. When complete bodies *are* found, they are in catastrophic death poses, indicating they died in a catastrophic event, and deposited in sea ecosystems. The fossil record points to a marine cataclysmic event rather than gradual processes.

The actual layers in the geological column are consistent with what would happen when flowing water filled with sediments starts to slow down. The various sediments settle in layers according to their weight and density; similar particles layer together. This is why we see sandstone and limestone close together in the various layers.

One might ask, "What evidence left behind gives us clues indicating whether this layering happened over a long or short time period?" One indication for rapid burial is that some sediment layers contain minerals that can weather away quickly when exposed to the environment. For example, in the San Francisco area beds of sediment hundreds of feet thick contain minerals such as manganese and phosphorite that typically would have eroded away if they had not been laid down and covered rapidly. Similar beds are found around the globe.

Alan V. Jopling of the Department of Geology at Harvard University is an expert regarding rapid burial. He states, "It is reasonable to postulate a very rapid rate of deposition; that is a single lamina [layer] would probably be deposited in a period of seconds or minutes rather than in a period of hours....There is factual evidence from both field observation and experiment that laminate composed of bed material are commonly deposited by current action within a period of seconds or minutes."

There is no evidence of erosion *between* the fossil layers, as one would expect if the sediment layering was a gradual process. There is no evidence of animals digging or burrowing in the layers, or of plant root systems in these layers. We find dinosaur tracks on the tops of layers, indicating they were soft or muddy when the prints were laid down, and then covered shortly after the tracks were laid. These tracks are found on top of layers but not in the middle of layers. Since the tracks are preserved, they have been covered by the next sediment layer shortly after they were laid down. The tracks have been discovered when a covering layer is removed. These tracks would have eroded away if they had been exposed to the elements over a long period of time. Most of the dinosaur footprints that have been found appear to be running uphill, as if the animals were fleeing to higher ground to outrun a flood. We find ripple marks on the tops of layers which may indicate water currents flowing over the layer shortly after it was laid down.

Human footprints have reportedly been found along with the dinosaur footprints. Secularists claim they are faked; we have only the integrity of the discoverer to validate the find.

One such set reportedly was found in Glen Rose, Texas, where I have seen what appeared to be a human footprint adjacent to a dinosaur footprint in cretaceous rock along the Cross Branch River. In 1995 human footprints were reportedly found in Turkmenistan. Kurban Amanniyazov, a local scientist, led three expeditions to the dinosaur plateau and found human footprints alongside dinosaur tracks, and he notes that "...if we speak about this human footprint, it was made by a human or a human like animal. Incredibly, this footprint is on the same plateau where there are dinosaur tracks. We can say the age of the footprint is not 5 or 10, but at least 150 million years old. It is 26 cm long, which is Russian size 43 (size 9.5 US) and we consider that whoever left the footprint was taller than we are." Russian experts investigated and verified the findings.

Amanniyazov concludes, "The implications of these discoveries are staggering: that human and dinosaur footprints are together at 2 sites is a pedestal smashing blow to evolutionism; the fact that Russian and Turkmenistan scientists have identified the human footprints is evidence that is hard to dismiss; another decisive blow to evolutionary theory are the goat tracks with human and dinosaur tracks. All these tracks are in the same Jurassic layer supposedly 200 million years old. This evidence wrecks the flimsy evolutionary time scale and would make any paleontologist pale." (livingdinos.com, Cryptozoology research team)

Rapid layering associated with water flow can be observed today, but the sediments laid down do not turn to rock. If there are sea creatures buried in layers today, why don't *they* turn into fossils? Under what conditions does fossilization happen? We know fossilization requires a quick burial and the right conditions. The sediments in the fossil record likely hardened because there were significant amounts of minerals and salt in the water and the sediment started to dry out soon after they were buried. The Bible indicates a great deal of water came from under the earth's surface in the flood—this water would likely be rich in salt, calcium, and other minerals.

There is still more evidence indicating rapid sediment layering. In various places around the globe we find sequences of strata that are bent or warped. This is commonly observed along roadways cut through mountains. This bending or warping continues through several layers, and would indicate that the rock was still pliable at the time the layers formed. If the rock layers were hard at the time, they would not be able to bend without fracturing.

Scientists holding the uniformitarian view believe the rock at some time became very hot and the heat allowed pressure to cause the rock to bend. However, if this heating had truly occurred, sedimentary rock would turn into metamorphic rock, just as limestone turns into marble. The heat would have destroyed any fossils inside that rock. But this is not the case since we observe bent limestone containing fossils.

Geologic formations such as rifts, folds, faults, and thrusts exist in all layers of strata, adding to the evidence that the sediment layers were pliable at the time the folding occurred—again pointing to rapid burial.

The fossils themselves yield more evidence of rapid burial. Fish have been fossilized while eating other fish. One fish was fossilized while giving birth. These fossils likely formed during catastrophic mudslides that buried the creatures quickly. Mudslides would be caused by huge tsunamis resulting from earthquakes under the surface of the earth. If the earth was covered in water, as the Bible describes in the global flood account, the tidal pull of the moon would have increased the usual tides into larger tidal waves. These waves would deposit sediment and debris, then recede, allowing for time to solidify between layering mudslides.

An Experiment You Can Do

To test this idea, mix sand and water together and add a significant amount of Epsom salt. Place the mixture in a small hole in dirt, and see what happens after a few days. Conduct a control test with sand but no salt. The salted sand will harden while the unsalted sand will not. This explanation fits the observed evidence of layers hardened into sedimentary rock.

More Evidence for a Worldwide Flood

The evidence for a worldwide catastrophic flood increases with each new geological discovery. Many modern geologists are beginning to accept limited catastrophism, or many catastrophic local floods over long time periods, which they say helps explain the fossil record. However, they still resist the idea of one worldwide flood.

One might ask, "What evidence (and in what places) could we expect to observe evidence of a worldwide flood like the Bible describes?" The highest mountain in the world, at 29,028 feet, is Mount Everest. Fossils of sea creatures in sedimentary rock have been found at its peak. Clams were found in the closed position, an indication of rapid burial, since they naturally pop open when they die unless they are buried quickly while still alive. The clams at the top of Mount Everest were closed, and hundreds of them were found in one four-cubic-foot space. This suggests they were dumped there during a catastrophic flood event. Secular science will say that millions of years ago Mt. Everest was under water, but they are unable to explain how the clams were buried all together and in the closed position indicating sudden and rapid burial.

There are also rock layers that run all the way across continents, some even beyond continents. These appear to have been laid down in one global event, not by a local flood or a river. There are many good examples of this, including Tapeats Sandstone and Redwall Limestone layers found in the Grand Canyon. Both run across the entire United States, into Canada, and even across the Atlantic Ocean to England.

Another example is the white cliffs of Dover. These are sedimentary chalk beds that run across Europe and down into the Middle East. This same layer is found in the Midwestern United States and in Western Australia. Obviously, local flooding cannot explain this; the evidence of the sedimentary rock layers points to a catastrophic worldwide flood event.

Often there is a long distance between where the sediment apparently originated and where it was laid down after it was eroded, offering more evidence of a large scale flood. For example, the Coconino Sandstone in the Grand Canyon was apparently picked up by rapidly moving water from its source in Canada and laid down hundreds of miles to the south.

Polystrate fossils pose another problem for the gradualist. These run through many levels of geological stratum and are found throughout the fossil record. Most are fossilized trees or tree trunks that extend through many layers, supposedly representing hundreds of thousands of years of stratum. These trees have been broken off at the roots, and often are found near coal-bearing strata. Some fossilized creatures are also in this area of polystrate fossils. Whales and other large sea creatures are found fossilized through many layers. Logic tells us that these large bodies don't stay around for thousands of years as the gradualists assume. Rapid burial and rapid layering again are the logical explanation.

Gradualists believe that coal was formed over millions of years as peat moss sank down into a swampy bog. A detective should ask, "Is this consistent with the evidence?"

The coal we find is clean, without the debris one would expect to find from a swamp. There is a great deal of coal buried in many areas around the world. What does the evidence tell us about how the coal beds came to be as they are today? A catastrophic global flood would pull up the trees by their roots. These trees and plants would form huge log mats buried in sedimentary rock, forming coal. We know from experiments today that when wood is confined under the right amount of heat and pressure, coal forms quickly.

Some hold that there is too much coal for this to have been laid down in a little over a year. In the fossil record, there is evidence that vegetation and plants were much larger than they are now. For instance, club mosses today reach heights of 16 to 18 inches, while in the fossil record they approach 200 feet tall. Fossilized trees almost 900 feet in length have been found; the tallest redwoods we have today are less than 400 feet. The fossilized trees found running through several layers of strata (found near the coal beds) would be the shorter trees pulled up by the roots and broken as they are caught up in the log mat near their burial point. They are often still upright, but without their roots.

Human artifacts, such as a manmade brass bell with an iron clapper, an iron pot, a gold chain, and bowls have been found embedded in coal fields (Morrisonville Illinois Times, June 11, 1891, among others). Gradualists who reject the catastrophic worldwide flood have no explanation for this evidence that humans were around before the coal was formed.

Does oil take millions of years to form? Not necessarily. Scientists have observed oil forming rapidly on the sea floor. Science has been able to produce oil in a few minutes under the right conditions in a laboratory. Oil formation requires the right pressure, water, hydrocarbons, and heat. The earth is filled with hydrocarbons, and deep in the earth we find pressure, heat, and water so we would expect to find oil in the earth. Oil explorers have gone back to old oil wells that were pumped dry, and in many cases find new oil, indicating that oil is continually forming and might even be classified as a limited renewable resource.

The fossil record evidence is what we would expect to observe after a catastrophic flood with huge waves and tsunamis. Often the simpler creatures are found at the bottom of the fossil layers, since they would be the first to be buried in their natural habitat. Those buried later, in a higher layer, would be the more mobile and intelligent sea creatures such as fish. As the waters rose and sediment deposits continued, the next to be buried would be the land creatures—the more mobile and intelligent would have avoided burial the longest by retreating to higher levels. Large animals and humans would float away as their bodies bloat and float after drowning. Body parts from animals would be found, but not many intact bodies. Bodies would only be intact if they were rapidly buried under sediment. The last to be buried of the dense bodies would be the birds, because they were able to fly to higher ground than the others. This scenario is consistent with what we find in the fossil record.

One might ask, "Don't dinosaurs prove the fossil record is old?" We have all been taught dinosaur bones are 65 to 75 million years old. No fossilized dinosaur bones show evidence of being chewed by predators. Most bones found are in poor condition and appear to have been either broken or damaged in some traumatic way.

Dinosaurs, as their name indicates, were "terrible lizards." Before the flood, the Bible tells us there was a water canopy over the earth, limiting radiation. The Biblical account states that people lived much longer then, possibly due to the lack of radiation reaching the earth. Animals lived much longer as well and, unlike humans and mammals, lizards continue to grow as they age—they never reach a full mature size and never stop growing. If lizards lived for hundreds of years, they would likely continue to grow to the size of the fossilized dinosaurs we find evidence of today. These same dinosaurs would have survived in the ark (a pair of adolescents) but would never reach the size of their pre-flood ancestors, and eventually became extinct before the present time. These are often known as dragons in ancient writings. Native American petroglyphs and other drawings include easily recognizable drawings of known dinosaur types. Native American oral traditions speak of people living with the dinosaurs. In the most ancient writings we have from China, the only animal mentioned is the dragon. Thus, the preponderance of evidence shows that men and dinosaurs lived together before the flood and for a time after as well.

More evidence comes from Dr. Mary Schweitzer, a paleontologist, who was one of the first scientists to discover soft tissue—blood vessels, proteins, various blood cells, and even DNA—inside fossilized dinosaur bones. If these bones were 65 million years old, they should not still contain soft tissue. But this finding would be possible and even expected if the animals were buried in the flood less than 4,500 years ago.

Schweitzer's research was received with extreme skepticism from the scientific community. She was told her specimens were likely contaminated, so she repeated the process 17 times, confirming that there was no contamination. The skeptics asked for DNA tests to see if the substance was from an animal or from bacterial contamination. She agreed and sent the substance off to be tested for DNA. The results came back that the tissue was in fact from animal origin.

The presence of soft tissue and DNA points to a much younger age than 65-75 million years. Many others have repeated similar tests, with the same results—proving the soft tissue retrieved from the fossilized bones is actually from dinosaurs. However, skeptics remain skeptical. In a Discover magazine article reporting Dr. Mary Schweitzer's discovery, she describes how one reviewer told her he didn't care what the data said, he knew that what she was finding wasn't possible. She wrote back and said, "Well, what data would convince you?" And he said, "None." It would appear some in the secular science world are not interested in evidence and truth.

Bob Enyart, a creationist with a daily radio talk show on KLTT in Denver, reached out to Dr. Schweitzer to suggest they conduct Carbon-14 dating on the soft tissue. He offered to pay for the testing and also make a $20,000 donation to her research group. Unfortunately, the scientists didn't want to give any more ammunition to the creationists beyond what they had already. The conversation between Enyart and Dr. Jack Horner, an associate of Dr. Schweitzer, is posted on YouTube.

Another soft tissue discovery came from the Hell Creek Formation excavation site in Montana where research scientist Mark Armitage from California State University discovered what he believed to be the largest triceratops horn ever unearthed. Upon examination of the horn under a high-powered microscope, Armitage was fascinated to find soft tissue in the sample. This discovery stunned members of the school's biology department, as the article explains, "…because it indicates that dinosaurs roamed the earth only thousands of years in the past rather than going extinct 60 million years ago." Shortly after Dr. Armitage published news of his original soft tissue discovery, a university official told Armitage, "We are not going to tolerate your religion in this department!" Armitage, a published scientist of over 30 years, was subsequently let go from the university. He later was reinstated through a lawsuit.

Recently, scientists have found a fossilized Spinolestes, a tiny rat like mammal that was believed to have lived 125 million years ago in what is now Spain. It had been exquisitely preserved as a fossil with hair, spine, and lung and liver tissues (Oct 14, 2015, Sciencemag.org).

Unfortunately, fossils do not come with dates, as we are reminded by Henry Gee, British paleontologist and evolutionary biologist: "No fossil is buried with its birth certificate. That and the scarcity of fossils, means that it is effectively impossible to link fossils into chains of cause and effects in any valid way....To take a line of fossils and claim that they represent a lineage is not a scientific hypothesis that can be tested, but an assertion that carries the same validity as a bedtime story—amusing, perhaps even instructive, but not scientific." (In Search of Deep Time— Beyond the Fossil Record to a New History of Life, (2010), pp. 116-117)

Radioisotope Dating

Radioisotope dating is one of the tools that gradualists use to validate their estimates of "millions and billions" of years. Radioisotope dating primarily links time to the process of potassium degrading to argon, uranium degrading to lead, thorium degrading to lead, samarium degrading to neodymium and rubidium degrading to strontium.

Sedimentary rock and fossils themselves cannot be dated by radioisotope dating; the technique can only be used to date the igneous rock (hardened lava) occasionally found between layers in the fossil record—the date is an indication of when the lava hardened.

Radioisotope dating makes three assumptions:

1) The rate of decay has been constant.
2) The quantity of parent or daughter atoms were known at the time the rock formed (for example uranium was 100 percent present when the rock was solidified and there was 0% lead present at that time).
3) No outside influence has affected the decay rate, no parent or daughter elements were lost or gained, and nothing affected the rate at any time.

Secular science has never calibrated calculated dates with actual known dates of igneous rocks. Instead the age is based on index fossils in the level near where they are found. And these dates are based on the assumptions of Charles Lyell.

In police work, our policy was always to calibrate our radar gun with a tuning fork before we used it. If it did not show the right speed, the radar unit could not be used.

Imagine that you are stopped by a police officer for speeding even though you were sure you had not done anything wrong. You begin recording the encounter with your phone camera. The police officer says his radar indicated you were speeding; you ask to see his radar device. You then ask him to calibrate it, and the calibration shows the radar is not operating properly. If the officer didn't void the ticket, and you showed your video to the press, the judge, or the police supervisor, there would be outrage. The officer would certainly lose his job and perhaps be charged with a crime. But what if no one cared and the police supervisors, the judge, and the media all took the side of the police officer with the faulty radar? That would indicate gross dishonesty and corruption.

This is essentially the case when it comes to commonly accepted methods for dating rocks. Instead of calibrating from rocks of known ages, geologists have assumed the different fossil layers were each a certain very old age. The assumption is made that the rocks the fossils are found in are that age as well. From a philosophical viewpoint this would be classified as circular reasoning. Legitimate testing of an unknown fossil requires calibration from a known dated rock.

The fallacy of this dating method used today is evident to W.D. Stansfield, Ph.D. Biology Professor at California Polytech State University: "All the above methods for dating the age of the earth, its various strata, and its fossils are questionable, because the rates are likely to have fluctuated widely over earth history....It is obvious that radiometric techniques may not be the absolute dating methods that they are claimed to be. Age estimates on a given geological stratum by different radiometric methods are often quite different (sometimes by hundreds of millions of years). There is no absolutely reliable long-term radiological 'clock'. The uncertainties inherent in radiometric dating are disturbing to geologists and evolutionists..." (Science of Evolution, Macmillan, pp. 82-84)

Michael Oard, Ph.D., a meteorologist and creation scientist, writes, "And when it comes to dating any individual rock today, the resulting 'date' is forced to conform to predetermined evolutionist 'dates' based on these imaginary 19th century index-fossil 'dates.' Any radiometric dates that show a supposedly 'old' rock to be young are rejected for no other reason. Few people realize that the index fossil dating system, despite its poor assumptions and many problems, is actually the primary dating tool for geologic time....In other words, radiometric dating methods are actually fit into the geological column, which was set up by [index] fossil dating over 100 years ago."

Igneous rocks with a known and observed formation age have been tested by radioisotope dating to shed light on the validity of the practice. In June 1992, geologist Dr. Steve Austin collected samples of dacite from the far north slope of the lava dome of Mount St. Helen's, a volcano that erupted twelve years earlier in 1980. The samples, which he knew had formed in 1980, came back with dates of 340,000 to 2.8 million years old. Rocks from Kilauea volcano, Hawaii were date tested; this had erupted less than 200 years ago but the test indicated the rocks were 22 million years old. Rocks from the volcano Hualalai in Hawaii that erupted in 1800 tested to be 160 million to 3.3 billion years old. Volcanic rocks formed only a few decades ago at Mt. Ngauruhoe in New Zealand were tested by various dating methods and purported to be anywhere from 270 thousand to 3.9 billion years old. When radioisotope dating fails to give accurate dates on rocks of known age, how can it be trusted to test rocks of an unknown age?

Additionally, the decay rate of rocks likely is not constant, as we see from a 2012 Popular Science magazine article, "Strange, Unexplained Solar Influence over Earth's Radioactive Material Could Herald Solar Flares." The article states, "This all goes back to 2006, when physicists at Purdue, Stanford and other places noticed something that at first defied physical explanation: Radioactive elements were changing their decay rates. This flew in the face of long-accepted physics theory, which held that these rates are constant. Radioactive decay apparently grew more pronounced in winter than in summer." This challenges the assumption that decay rates are constant.

Carbon 14 dating

Carbon 14 is a dating method developed in the 1950s and is considered to be accurate back 60,000 to 100,000 years. Living things take in radioactive C14 until they die. At this point, C14 starts to decay, with a half-life (meaning half of it is depleted) of 5,734 years. Certain assumptions are built into C14 dating; one being that the level of C14 in the atmosphere has been constant. (If there was a worldwide flood, the C14 levels could have been much lower at the time.) The second assumption is the decay rate has remained constant.

Since dinosaurs were thought to be 65 to 200 million years old, carbon dating was never used to test their age until recently. Members of the Paleochronology group presented their findings at the 2012 Western Pacific Geophysics Meeting in Singapore, August 13-17, a conference of the American Geophysical Union (AGU) and the Asia Oceania Geosciences Society (AOGS). Members of the Paleochronology group sent samples of dinosaur bones for C14 testing. They got back dates that ranged from 22,000 to 39,000 years old, not millions of years. These are still older than one would expect given a flood scenario, but that could be explained by lower C14 levels before or during the flood. Regardless, it is further evidence that dinosaurs are not millions of years old.

C14 dating has proven unreliable as an accurate measure of age. A sample taken from a living penguin showed it had died 8,000 years ago. The shells of living mollusks dated using the C14 method tested as having been dead for 23,000 years. The remains of a seal dead for 30 years was carbon dated as 4,600 years old.

A team from the Institute for Creation Research RATE team (Radioisotopes and the Age of the Earth) obtained coal samples from the U.S. Department of Energy Coal Bank. The samples were from the top, middle, and bottom of the coal bed, which supposedly represented different time periods in the geologic column (Cenozoic, Mesozoic, and Paleozoic ages). The coal samples were sent for C14 testing and all were found to have significant and similar levels of C14. The uniformitarian model holds the coal fields formed over long periods of time, millions of years ago. The carbon 14 levels were consistent with thousands of years, not millions.

The RATE group also checked for Carbon 14 in diamonds mined from deep within the earth. The uniformitarian model suggests diamonds were formed at the very beginning of the formation of the earth, billions of years ago. The diamonds had significant levels of C14, consistent with an age of thousands of years, not millions or billions.

When we look at the evidence of the geological record with an open mind, the evidence for a worldwide catastrophic flood as the Bible records is overwhelming. What a wonderful position for a Christian to be in, rather than having to come up with outlandish explanations each time evidence is discovered!

Our Creator God wants us to find Him, and He is allowing more evidence of Himself and His past mighty works to be uncovered every day. The evidence of water being pent up and released shortly after the flood, and the evidence from the Ice Age, which most likely occurred just after the flood, all allow us to engage our mind in discovering what God has left behind, rather than putting our intellect in neutral to blindly accept gradualism and "millions of years."

What about the Grand Canyon?

What explanation for the Grand Canyon's formation best fits the observed evidence? It is possible and even reasonable to believe that the sedimentary layers found in the walls were laid down during the flood, before the canyon formed. As the flood waters dried up, there could have been a great deal of water (perhaps more than was left in the Great Lakes) trapped on the land at a slightly higher elevation. After the water pressure built up, the water would eventually break through the land holding it back, forming a spillway. The flood waters then would seek the path of least resistance, forming the canyon.

In contrast, the uniformitarian model says the Colorado River slowly cut through the mountain, forming the canyon over millions of years. However, where the river enters the canyon, the canyon's top elevation is 6,000 feet and it flows through an area with rock walls up to 9,000 feet high, called the Kaibaab plateau, before coming down again. Uniformitarian geologists tell us the river was flowing through the area before the land rose. But we know the rising land would have diverted the river. Indeed, geologists have found evidence that ancient rivers in the area flowed in the opposite direction, towards the northeast, suggesting that the plateau predated the river and the river isn't millions of years old.

Another difficult question for the uniformitarian is, "At what elevation in the side of the Canyon did the river start cutting or eroding the rock?" We see evidence of cutting all the way to the top layers. If the river started eroding the sides of the Canyon before all the layers were laid down, there would be no sharp cut-off above it. If the river started eroding the rock after all the layers were laid, it would take too much time to erode down the whole canyon. If slow moving rivers cut canyons, why are there not canyons around every river? If the Canyon was carved slowly by the Colorado River, where is the river delta? And where are the rocks that once filled this huge canyon? Did they suddenly disappear?

There is a small delta at the mouth but it is not consistent with all the material from the canyon. I am confident the best explanation of the circumstance that led to the Grand Canyon is a post or late flood event where the water built up and then suddenly flowed out with tremendous force, following the path of least resistance.

Recent Rapidly Formed Canyons

There is evidence of a similar canyon forming after the eruption of Mount St. Helen on May 18, 1980. The eruption was localized but enormous. In six minutes it leveled 150 square miles of forest. A "Little Grand Canyon" formed in one day from a mudflow that broke through volcanic debris and ash that had blocked the north fork of the Toutle River. The pressure from the released water carved a canyon 150 feet long, 100 feet deep, and nearly 200 feet wide. Layers were observed to form in hours and days, not millions of years.

Another example of a rapidly formed canyon is Canyon Lake Gorge, formed in 2002. At one point a great deal of rain fell around Canyon Lake, Texas and when a dam in the area threatened to burst, officials released water through a spillway. In just three days this overflow of water formed a huge canyon through solid sedimentary rock, which shocked geologists. It blew out 1.3 miles of rock 23 feet deep.

Fast flowing water is truly powerful. According to Nature Geoscience magazine, "Our traditional view of deep river canyons, such as the Grand Canyon, is that they are carved slowly as the regular flow and occasionally moderate running of eroded rocks over periods of millions of years; such is not always the case."

Finally, here is one more example of rapid canyon formation—the Burlingame Canyon near Walla Walla, Washington formed in six days. In March 1926, tumbleweeds blocked an irrigation channel near there and high water levels from spring rains caused water to back up. To clean out the obstruction, engineers diverted the flow into a ditch feeding into nearby Pine Creek. The ditch was rather small, no greater than 10 feet deep and 6 feet wide, and often no water flowed through it at all. But the abnormally high flow of fast water formed the canyon, now 120 feet deep and 120 feet wide.

Final Thoughts

Only a small portion of the evidence for the Biblical flood has been covered in this chapter. I hope it leads you to think for yourself and consider all the evidence regarding scientific matters, even when mainstream science seems to predetermine the answer and ridicule feasible alternatives. Ravi Zacharias points out the problem: "Ultimately, the problem with man is not the absence of evidence; it is the suppression of it."

The evidence leads us to trust the Genesis record as a true account of a worldwide flood. This will cause you to look at the world differently. I did not address all the questions you may have in this chapter but I encourage you to do your own detective work. There are creation ministries that will likely have the answers that I didn't cover. Creation International Ministries (creation.com), The Institute for Creation Research (icr.org), and Answers in Genesis (answersingenesis.org) are a few.

Chapter Five

Darwinian Evolution

"Wisdom is supreme, so get wisdom. And whatever else you get, get understanding."

-Proverbs 4:7

"It is the glory of God to conceal a matter; to search out a matter is the glory of kings."

-Proverbs 25:2

"But test all things. Hold on to what is good."

-1 Thessalonians 5:21

"I am against religion because it teaches us to be satisfied with not understanding the world."

-Richard Dawkins

Early in my police career I was trained as an accident investigator and reconstruction specialist with the Houston Police Department. By examining skid marks, yaw marks, debris, vehicle damage, and any other evidence at the scene, and applying the mathematical formulas I had been taught, I was able to reconstruct the events of an accident even though I had not actually seen it occur. I was trained to look at the effects and determine from the evidence how the accident was caused.

One night I was called to the scene of a police car accident. I took the statement from the officer about what happened and then looked at the evidence. The officer told me the other driver was intoxicated and I was able to confirm that fact. However, the story the officer gave didn't match up with the evidence at the scene, including the positioning of the cars, the debris, and the skid marks. I called another experienced investigator and a supervisor to come by to back me up.

During that time a call went out on the police radio for a supervisor to go to a nearby convenience store. There the supervisor found an eyewitness to the accident who had been ordered to leave the accident scene by the officer involved and was threatened with arrest. Regardless, the witness wanted to tell us what he saw. Eventually I interviewed this witness and his story contradicted the police officer's but lined up completely with the evidence at the accident scene.

Apparently the officer was driving down the street early in morning when there was very little traffic. He decided to ignore a four-way stop at a rather high speed. Unfortunately, another car at the intersection pulled out in front of him and he was unable to avoid a collision. The officer laid down long skid marks and ran into the side of the car. When he noticed the driver of the other vehicle was intoxicated, he tried to change the scene, moving the cars and blaming the accident on the other driver. He got some vehicles to park on top of his skid marks to cover them up but I saw them anyway. I put all this information in my report and submitted it. The officer eventually lost his job because of what he did that night.

Looking at Evolution

When I look at the evidence for evolution, I feel like I did the night of that accident. The story told by secular science does not match up with the evidence. In this chapter I will submit my report and my conclusions based on looking at the evidence. I am going to report it like I see it, as I did that night on the street. I will also call in experts to back me up.

Academia knows there are problems with evolution but they are not talking about it, as confirmed by Professor Jerome Lejeune, a French pediatrician and geneticist. In a lecture in Paris on March 17, 1985, he said, "We have no acceptable theory of evolution at the present time. There is none; and I cannot accept the theory that I teach to my students each year. Let me explain. I teach the synthetic theory known as the neo-Darwinian one, for one reason only; not because it's good, we know that it is bad, but because there isn't any other. Whilst waiting to find something better you are taught something which is known to be inexact."

However, a few brave scientists are publicly admitting what they have known privately for years—the evolution theory has real problems. Most professors today know evolution has many absurd assumptions and unanswerable questions, but the majority will never admit it; if they do, their jobs, their chance of getting published, and their grant money will be at risk. Students who express doubts about evolution will likely see their grades or recommendations suffer.

Definition of Evolution

Evolution is defined by Webster's World Dictionary of Science (edited by evolutionary scientists) as "The slow process of change from one form to another. Organic evolution traces the development of simple unicellular forms to more complex (advanced, i.e. better) forms ..."

In his book, <u>On The Origin of Species</u>, (1859), Charles Darwin shows that species have changed over time, and he explains how natural selection produces such change. Darwin doesn't define a "species," explain how they came to be as we see them, or describe how new species emerged, other than to imply natural selection was responsible.

The Roots of Evolution, the Fossil Record

As noted earlier, Darwin was influenced by the conclusions Charles Lyell reached based on the fossil record. The idea of humans evolving from primordial soup to sea creatures, then coming onto land and evolving to mankind is similar to ancient pagan myths. This story likely started with Lyell.

The influence of Lyell on Darwin's thinking cannot be overestimated. Referring to his voyage on the Beagle (1831–1836), in <u>Beagle Diary</u> (p. 27) Darwin writes, "I had brought with me the first volume of Lyell's <u>Principles of Geology</u>, which I studied attentively; and this book was of the highest service to me in many ways." Darwin writes in his memoirs (Barlow, 1958: p. 101), "The science of Geology is enormously indebted to Lyell—more so, as I believe, than to any other man who ever lived."

Lyell's <u>Principles of Geology</u> prompted Darwin to assume the slow evolutionary process was true, since long periods of time and slow change were critical to Lyell's interpretation of the fossil record.

We saw in the previous chapter how the old age of the fossil record is not supported by the evidence. Yet this fossil record is still touted as evidence for the billions of years necessary for evolution to have occurred. S.M. Stanley, paleontologist and evolutionary biologist at the University of Hawaii at Mano, explains the importance of the fossil record to the evolutionary theory in his book <u>The New Evolutionary Timetable</u> (p. 95): "It is doubtful whether, in the absence of fossils, the idea of evolution would represent anything more than an outrageous hypothesis....The fossil record and only the fossil record provide direct evidence of major sequential changes in the Earth's biota."

Similarly, Carl O. Dunbar, Ph.D. (Geology) Professor of Paleontology and Stratigraphy, Yale University, in his book <u>Historical Geology</u> (p. 47) says, "Fossils provide the only historical, documentary evidence that life has evolved from simpler to more and more complex forms."

However, Darwin knew the conclusions he drew from the fossil record were problematic. He hoped the lack of evidence for "transitional forms" would be solved by future discoveries. As he says in <u>Origins</u> (p. 292), "The number of intermediate varieties which have formerly existed on earth must be truly enormous. Why then is not every geological formation and every stratum full of such intermediate links? Geology assuredly does not reveal any such finely graduated organic chain; and this, perhaps, is the most obvious and gravest objection which can be urged against my theory."

Darwin surely would be disappointed to know that we are still waiting to find solid evidence for transitional forms in the fossil record. Granted, within the fossil record we do see different species emerge and disappear, but without evidence of any major changes, such as an arm changing to a wing.

Darwinian believers claim to have found some of these transitional forms, but in reality what Darwin said back then is still true today: there is no evidence for macro-evolution in the fossil record.

This is verified by Dr. David M. Raup, a paleontologist at the University of Chicago: "The evidence we find in the geologic record is not nearly as compatible with Darwinian natural selection as we would like it to be. Darwin was completely aware of this. He was embarrassed by the fossil record because it didn't look the way he predicted it would....Well, we are now about 120 years after Darwin and the knowledge of the fossil record has been greatly expanded. We now have a quarter of a million fossil species but the situation hasn't changed much...ironically, we have even fewer examples of evolutionary transition than we had in Darwin's time. By this I mean that some of the classic cases of Darwinian change in the fossil record, such as the evolution of the horse in North America, have had to be discarded or modified as the result of more detailed information." The evidence just isn't there. The more the fossil record is investigated, the more information we have that Darwin's theory does not match up with the evidence.

In a personal letter to a colleague, Dr. Colin Patterson, Senior Paleontologist at the British Museum of Natural History, recognized this problem, stating, "...I fully agree with your comments on the lack of direct illustration of evolutionary transition in my book. If I knew of any, fossil or living, I would certainly have included them....Yet Gould and the American Museum people are hard to contradict when they say there are no transitional fossils....I will lay it on the line—there is not one such fossil for which one could make a watertight argument....It is easy enough to make up stories of how one form gave rise to another....But such stories are not part of science, for there is no way of putting them to the test....I don't think we shall ever have any access to any form of tree which we can call factual."

The missing links and the transitional forms are still missing. Dr. Scott Huse, in his book, The Collapse of Evolution, cleverly points out this problem. "Faith is the substance of fossils hoped for, the evidence of links unseen." Even if one accepts the assumption of long ages, the fossil record still does not provide evidence for macro-evolution as Darwin proposed.

Looking at the Evidence as a Detective Would

A detective should follow the evidence wherever it leads. In contrast, it seems as though Darwin accepted the uniformitarian worldview as true and then set out on his voyage to validate this conclusion. Author A.C. Doyle understood this inherent problem, when he said, through his

109

character Sherlock Holmes, "It's a capital mistake to theorize before one has data. Insensibly, one begins to twist facts to suit theories instead of theories to suit facts."

This is exactly what Darwin did. Dr. Barry Gale (Science Historian, Darwin College, UK) explains in his book, Evolution without Evidence: "[Darwin's] theory had, in essence, preceded his knowledge—that is, he had hit upon a novel and evocative theory of evolution with limited knowledge at hand to satisfy either he or others that the theory was true. He could neither accept it himself nor prove it to others. He simply did not know enough concerning the several natural history fields upon which his theory would have to be based."

When Darwin set out on his voyage to the Galapagos Islands, he had no formal training in either biology or paleontology. His training was in theology. In a letter to his friend Asa Gray, Darwin admitted that his theory was very speculative: "I am quite conscious that my speculations run beyond the bounds of true science....It is a mere rag of an hypothesis with as many flaw[s] & holes as sound parts." However, his evolution "speculations" have never been characterized as such; his theory was taught at the time as if it was factual and it is taught as settled science by most in the scientific community today.

On his journey, the main evidence Darwin pointed to in order to validate his theory was the variation in the sizes of finches' beaks. On islands where the nuts had harder and thicker shells he found the finches had larger beaks. Darwin concluded from this that originally there were two finches that migrated to the islands. From these two, offspring

110

evolved to have the different beaks on the different islands where they ended up. He extrapolated this evidence to validate Lyell's hypothesis of how we evolved from primordial soup.

In fact, a closer look at finch beaks reveals that the beak sizes change back and forth based on changing environmental conditions, consistent with *adaptation* rather than permanent change. The appropriate question is, "Is it the hardness of the nuts that causes the change in the beaks, or built in design?" I believe the changes are part of the finches' design and are God's way of allowing them to adapt to various environments. The important thing to note is these birds still remain finches, so to say this is evidence that one species evolves from another is intellectually dishonest to the highest degree.

Assumptions of Evolution

Every scientific theory has some assumptions. Darwinian Evolution certainly has ideas that are accepted without proof. G. A. Kerkut, a British biologist, published a book entitled Implications of Evolution where he lists seven assumptions implicit in the theory of evolution:

1) Life arose from nonliving matter (i.e., spontaneous generation occurred).
2) Spontaneous generation only occurred once.
3) Viruses, bacteria, plants and animals are interrelated.
4) Multicellular animals...evolved from unicellular or single-celled organisms (protozoa or protists).
5) Various invertebrate phyla are interrelated.

111

6) Vertebrate animals evolved from invertebrate animals.
7) Vertebrate animals evolved from fish to amphibians, from amphibians to reptiles, from reptiles to birds and mammals, etc.

It is important to acknowledge that a totally naturalistic worldview assumes much more than these seven occurrences. Another is that the fine tuning of the universe and the delicate conditions necessary for life came by time plus chance, as we discussed in Chapter 2. Evolutionists also assume the conditions in the universe were established and stable before life supposedly emerged from non-life, again thanks to time plus chance.

Leonard Susskind, cosmologist and father of the string theory, makes the following point in his book, The Cosmic Landscape (p. 343): "Our own universe is an extraordinary place that appears to be fantastically well designed for our own existence. This specialness is not something that we can attribute to lucky accidents, which is far too unlikely. The apparent coincidences cry out for an explanation." The evolutionists do not have an explanation for how the universe came to be as it is, just assumptions.

Back to the assumptions, we see Kerkut's assumptions are very problematic. Evolutionists would say the first two have nothing to do with Darwinian Evolution. I disagree. Darwin avoided discussing these matters as he knew they were problematic. But assuming a naturalistic worldview, one would have to assume life arrived from non-life by time plus chance. When evolutionists assume the supernatural has no part in past events, they are assuming that life must have spontaneously derived from non-life in the past.

Life from Non-life

The idea of life coming from non-life is contrary to the scientific Law of Biogenesis and cell theory. The Law of Biogenesis states that life can only come from life. The cell theory states that cells can only come from cells.

Two well-known scientists, Fred Hoyle and N. Chandra Wickramasinghe, in their book Evolution From Space, discuss the likelihood of life beginning by natural processes: "...life cannot have had a random beginning....The trouble is that there are about two thousand enzymes, and the chance of obtaining them all in a random trial is only one part in 10 to the 40,000 power, an outrageously small probability that could not be faced even if the whole universe consisted of organic soup. If one is not prejudiced either by social beliefs or by a scientific training into the conviction that life originated on the Earth, this simple calculation wipes the idea entirely out of court....The enormous information content of even the simplest living systems...cannot in our view be generated by what are often called 'natural' processes....For life to have originated on the Earth it would be necessary that quite explicit instruction should have been provided for its assembly....There is no way in which we can expect to avoid the need for information, no way in which we can simply get by with a bigger and better organic soup, as we ourselves hoped might be possible a year or two ago."

Thus, Hoyle and Wickramasinghe estimated that there is less than 1 chance in 10 to the 40,000th power that the 2,000 enzymes necessary for life could have originated by random chance. The odds for these enzymes coming together with the other functional organelles necessary to form a simple cell by chance has been put at 1 in 10 to the 340 millionth power! Mathematicians consider any odds greater than 1 in 10 to the 50th power to be impossible. No matter how much time and chance is added to the mix, the formation of a simple cell by natural means is impossible. Only a supernatural power could have caused it.

During the time of Darwin, it was not uncommon to believe life could emerge from non-life, a process called abiogenesis. After all, people observed mosquitoes arising spontaneously from ponds and maggots forming on meat, for example. But if they had a good microscope, they would have known this wasn't happening. Further, Darwin thought the cell was very simple, but now we know it is very complex. According to American biochemist Linus Pauling, "just one living cell in the human body is more complex than New York City." We know that all living things on earth are extremely complex; even the tiniest single-celled protozoa and bacteria are amazingly complicated.

Concerning abiogenesis, evolutionist agnostic Dr. Robert Jastrow, in his book Until the Sun Dies (pp. 62-63), says, "At present, science has no satisfactory answer to the question of the origin of life on the earth. Perhaps the appearance of life on the earth is a miracle. Scientists are reluctant to accept that view, but their choices are limited; either life was created on the earth by the will of a being outside the grasp of scientific understanding, or it evolved on our planet spontaneously, through chemical reactions occurring in nonliving matter lying on the surface of the planet. The first theory places the question of the origin of life beyond the reach of scientific inquiry. It is a statement of faith in the power of a Supreme Being not subject to the laws of science. The second theory is also an act of faith. The act of faith consists in assuming that the scientific view of the origin of life is correct, without having concrete evidence to support that belief."

The scientific case against abiogenesis was first made by scientist Francisco Ready in 1668. In various experiments, he proved that life cannot arise from non-living matter. His conclusions have never been disproved. However, the theory of abiogenesis gained new strength after Lyell introduced his theory of gradualism based on the fossil record. Darwin built on those assumptions, and spontaneous generation of life as a theory took root in the 19th century scientific community.

During this same time, scientist Louis Pasteur also was investigating the possibility of spontaneous generation of life. Pasteur scientifically concluded that life only comes from life and he called it the "Law of Biogenesis" in 1859. This, too, has never been proven wrong. Ironically this was the same year Darwin published On the Origin of the Species. Pasteur was an early and vocal critic of Darwin's work, but his Law of Biogenesis did not receive the attention that it warranted—it should have dealt a death blow to the idea of spontaneous generation of life. Darwin was careful to avoid mentioning spontaneous origin of life in his book, but it is still a necessary assumption in order for his naturalistic model to work.

In an attempt to resolve this dilemma, The Origin of Life Foundation is currently offering a $1 million prize to anyone who can provide a chemically plausible naturalistic solution for the origin of life and the genetic code. The organization's website (www.lifeorigin.org) states: "'The Origin-of-Life Prize' will be awarded for proposing a highly plausible mechanism for the spontaneous rise of genetic instructions in nature sufficient to give rise to life. To win, the explanation must be consistent with empirical biochemical, kinetic, and thermodynamic concepts as further delineated herein and be published in a well-respected, peer-reviewed science journal(s)." The announcement is in a private area of the Foundation's website accompanied by the following statement: "The Origin-of-Life Foundation, Inc. wishes to keep the project as quiet as possible within the scientific community."

Not one case of spontaneous generation of life has ever been observed; no realistic mechanism has ever been hypothesized. I believe the Foundation will be able to keep the prize money.

The Cell Theory

The cell theory states that cells can only be produced from other cells. Individual cells are incredibly complicated, continually performing innumerable complex biochemical reactions. Evolutionist Michael Denton explains, "The complexity of the simplest known type of cell is so great that it is impossible to accept that such an object could have been thrown together suddenly by some kind of freakish, vastly improbable, event. Such an occurrence would be indistinguishable from a miracle."

Scientist Fred Hoyle is in agreement on this point. He suggests that supposing the first cell originated by chance is like believing "a tornado sweeping through a junk yard might assemble a Boeing 747 from the materials therein."

The Second Evolution Assumption

The second assumption accepted by evolutionists is that life arose from non-life only during a short period of time a long time ago. This assumption says it can no longer happen now, but it did happen then. This is pure conjecture without a shred of evidence. There is no evidence of even the primordial soup they assume. Some naturalists attempt to explain the lack of evidence by saying all the evidence for early life forms was eaten up by later life forms. That is convenient but not very believable—and nothing more than wishful thinking.

The Remaining Evolution Assumptions

Evolutionists argue that Kerkut's final five assumptions noted above can be explained through the mechanisms of natural selection and random mutations, which we will cover later in this chapter. There are innumerable problems with cells coming together to form complex beings, and explaining how this can occur is a major challenge for evolutionists. Here are just a few of those problems.

Irreducible Complexity

Biochemistry professor Michael Behe introduced the idea of irreducible complexity using the bacterial flagella as an example. Its molecular motor requires 40 separate complex protein components. Behe states that the absence of any one of these proteins would make the flagella nonfunctional. Thus if the flagella engine were to be reduced in its complexity to earlier and simpler stages of its supposed evolutionary development, it would not be viable or functional. As it is designed, it spins at an amazing 100,000 RPMs and can reverse its direction within one quarter of a spin.

Darwin understood that irreducible complexity would raise questions about his theory. Even he questioned how the eye could have evolved by chance. In Origins (p. 217), he writes, "To suppose that the eye, with all its inimitable contrivances for adjusting the focus to different distances, for admitting different amounts of light, and for the correction of spherical and chromatic aberration, could have been formed by natural selection seems, I freely confess, absurd in the highest possible degree."

He goes on, though, to present a rather absurd model of how he believed eyes evolved from the primitive to the complex. The possibility that this happened by chance is problematic in many ways. A human eye has 130 million photoreceptor cells that work together in a very complicated way. In the animal kingdom, science has identified 30 different unique eye types with various special features. Each would have developed on a separate track if the evolution model was correct. Each is an example of irreducible complexity, since every one of them has highly organized structures and complicated mechanisms, and could not function or remain viable in transitional forms. The example of the eye remains a major problem for evolutionists. Suggesting that it came together by micro changes of chance and time is nothing more than fantasy.

The natural formation of the eye is only one problem; figuring out how eyes became connected to the brain is another. And beyond that, how did the brain itself form through a long series of gradual changes? While the eye is amazing, the human brain is even more incredible.

Stephen Smith, a professor of molecular and cellular physiology and one of the lead researchers in this area, reports that new images reveal the brain to be vastly more intricate than anyone had ever imagined. He concludes, "One synapse, by itself, is more like a microprocessor—with both memory-storage and information-processing elements—than a mere on/off switch. In fact, one synapse may contain on the order of 1,000 molecular-scale switches. A single human brain has more switches than all the computers and routers and Internet connections on Earth."

The design of the human brain is amazing beyond our comprehension. It contains 100 billion neurons, each connected to 10 thousand other neurons by 10 thousand miles of connective tissue. Man's three-pound brain is capable of storing and creatively processing seemingly infinite amounts of information. Its capabilities and potential stagger the imagination. The human brain is the most complicated object in the known universe. To suppose this came about by random chance and gradual changes over time is ludicrous.

We see this dilemma in an article from the evolutionist journal, <u>Nature</u>, 12 February 2009, "Darwin's bridge between microevolution and macroevolution" (<u>Nature</u>, Vol. 457, pp. 837-842) which states in part, "Darwin anticipated that microevolution would be a process of continuous and gradual change. The term macroevolution, by contrast, refers to the origin of new species and divisions of the taxonomic hierarchy above the species level, and also to the origin of complex adaptations, such as the vertebrate eye. Macroevolution posed a problem to Darwin because his principle of descent with modification predicts gradual transitions between small-scale adaptive changes in populations and these larger-scale phenomena, yet there is little evidence for such transitions in nature. Instead, the natural world is often characterized by gaps, or discontinuities. One type of gap relates to the existence of 'organs of extreme perfection', such as the eye, or morphological innovations, such as wings, both of which are found fully formed in present-day organisms without leaving evidence of how they evolved."

Natural Selection

The notion that natural selection was the driving force behind gradual changes in the past was Darwin's noted discovery and his claim to fame. Natural selection over long time periods is essential to Darwinian evolution theory.

Twenty-four years before Darwin used it, Edward Blyth (1810 to 1873) coined the term "natural selection."

Blyth was an English chemist and zoologist who wrote three major articles on natural selection which he saw as part of God's design—His way of maintaining the strength of different species. Blyth observed, for example, that the stronger male deer would win battles and then mate with the females of the herd, strengthening the genetic line through natural selection. He also believed the weaker and slower offspring would be captured first by predators, taking the unfit out of the genetic pool of the species by natural selection.

Blyth was a Christian creationist. He never claimed natural selection could transform one species into another or simple life forms into far more complex life, as Darwin did. Within Darwin's library, housed in the archives of Cambridge University, there are copies of the magazines that contain Blyth's articles, with Darwin's handwritten notes in the margins. It seems that Darwin took this reasonable theory proposed by Blyth and then twisted the concept of natural selection in an attempt to find a mechanism for Lyell's gradualism.

We can observe natural selection even today. But is it an explanation of the past evolution of simple forms to complex ones? Or is it a process designed by an intelligent Creator? Darwin studied dogs, cats, horses, donkeys, pigs, sheep, goats, rabbits, pigeons, many birds, goldfish, bees, beetles, silk moths, fruit trees, grains, culinary plants, and orchids. He found variations within a species, but no evidence of change from one species to another as a result of natural selection or any other mechanism.

Survival of the Fittest

"Survival of the fittest" was not originally a part of Darwin's concept of natural selection. The term came from biologist Herbert Spencer, who suggested to Darwin that natural selection would be better understood in those terms. Darwin used the phrase in his 5th edition of <u>Origins</u> (1869), to further clarify natural selection. Even if the general principle of survival of the fittest is valid, this still does not explain the initial "arrival" of the fittest.

Neo-Darwinian Evolution: Random Mutations

Survival of the fittest and natural selection are the only mechanisms Darwin proposed for his evolution model and they remain vitally important to his theory. Following Darwin's death, scientists knew Darwin's theory was lacking. After genes were discovered, evolutionists seized upon another mechanism to support their theory, a process known as "random mutations," which are integral to the "Neo-Darwinian evolution theory." This holds that random mutations and natural selection are sufficient mechanisms to explain evolutionary changes from simple to complex forms in the past.

Evolutionists hold that natural selection will weed out the bad mutations and allow the good mutations to flourish, resulting in consistently positive evolutionary changes.

Scientists knew very little about mutations at the time. We know now that mutations are copying errors that change the DNA code. They result in a variant form of the genetic information transmitted to subsequent generations.

Mutations can be naturally occurring copying errors or caused by exposure to radiation or chemicals. Bill Gates, founder of Microsoft, in the film "Programming of Life," says, "DNA is like a computer program, but far, far more advanced than any software we've ever created."

A good friend of mine is a senior programmer at a computer hardware company. He and his team spend months designing new programs to produce computer hardware. These programs tell the hardware how to operate, very much like DNA but much less complex. I asked him what would happen if after they completed their work, someone snuck in and typed in a small change to the program. What are the odds that it would cause a positive change and make the hardware even better than what it was designed to be? He responded, "Ha!" I explained he didn't understand the science behind evolution—if it happened enough times over millions of years it would have to eventually result in better hardware, right? His response: "Ha! Ha!" Apparently mutations are not so good when it comes to computer programs!

In his case, the program is the set of instructions for a computer function—just as DNA is a set of instructions for the assembly and function of parts within a cell. Darwin and his contemporaries did not know anything about DNA and its incredible complexity. A fundamental question for evolutionists continues to be: "How did the information get into DNA in the first place?"

George Sim Johnston, a free-lance writer, is quoted by Lee Strobel in <u>The Case for a Creator</u>, (p. 219) saying, "Human DNA contains more organized information than the

Encyclopedia Britannica. If the full text of the encyclopedia were to arrive in computer code from outer space, most people would regard this as proof of the existence of extraterrestrial intelligence. But when seen in nature, it is explained as the workings of random forces."

Mutations

Mutations result in a change in DNA, the hereditary information that determines what the organism will look like and how it will function. A change in an organism's DNA can cause changes in all aspects of its form and function. Neo-Darwinian evolution assumes that positive mutations can explain how primitive life forms evolved to where mankind is today. But one must ask: where is the evidence for advantageous mutations?

To validate the theory that positive macro change can occur through mutation, researchers in the early 20th century conducted an experiment using fruit flies. Fruit flies have a short gestation and are susceptible to frequent mutations so the researchers exposed the fruit flies to radiation and chemicals to trigger these mutations. A more extensive experiment with fruit flies was started in 1975 and completed in 2010. The results were headlined: "35 Year Mutation Study of Fruit Flies Fails Miserably." (Ref: Genome-wide analysis of a long-term evolution experiment with Drosophila; Nature, Vol. 467, pp. 587-590).

The article states, "This research really upends the dominant paradigm about how species evolve...as stated in regards to the 35-year experimental failure to fixate a single beneficial mutation within fruit flies." The article continues,

"They were able to produce over 1,500 generations of fruit flies during this experiment. Instead of waiting for natural selection to do its job, researchers used forced selection on hundreds of generations of fruit flies. They used variation to breed fruit flies that develop from egg to adult 20% faster than normal. But, as usual when breeding plants and animals, there was a down side. In this case the fruit flies weighed less, lived shorter lives, and were less resistant to starvation. There were many mutations, but none caught on, and the experiment ran into the limits of variation....Despite decades of sustained selection in relatively small, sexually reproducing laboratory populations, selection did not lead to the fixation of newly arising unconditionally advantageous alleles....The probability of fixation in wild populations should be even lower than its likelihood in these experiments."

Fruit flies remained fruit flies and did not evolve into anything else. The mutated flies were worse off than the original. None of the observed mutations were advantageous—the insects were not better equipped to survive in nature. Changes *were* observed, such as differently shaped wings and extra wings, but none made for a better fruit fly. As the article sums up, "Advantageous anatomical mutations are never observed. The four-winged fruit fly is a case in point: The second set of wings lacks flight muscles, so the useless appendages interfere with flying and mating, and the mutant fly cannot survive long outside the laboratory. Similar mutations in other genes also produce various anatomical deformations, but they are harmful, too."

In <u>Populations, Species, and Evolution</u> (p. 235) Harvard evolutionary biologist Ernst Mayr, states, "The occurrence of genetic monstrosities by mutation...is well substantiated, but they are such evident freaks that these monsters can be designated only as 'hopeless.' They are so utterly unbalanced that they would not have the slightest chance of escaping elimination through stabilizing selection...the more drastically a mutation affects the phenotype, the more likely it is to reduce fitness. To believe that such a drastic mutation would produce a viable new type, capable of occupying a new adaptive zone, is equivalent to believing in miracles...The finding of a suitable mate for the 'hopeless monster' and the establishment of reproductive isolation from the normal members of the parental population seem to me insurmountable difficulties."

Pierre-Paul Grasse (Past-President, French Acadamie des Sciences) in his book <u>Evolution of Living Organisms</u> (p. 103) confirms this problem: "The opportune appearance of mutations permitting animals and plants to meet their needs seems hard to believe. Yet the Darwinian Theory is even more demanding: a single plant, a single animal would require thousands and thousands of lucky, appropriate events. Thus, miracles would become the rule: events with an infinitesimal probability could not fail to occur....There is no law against day dreaming, but science must not indulge in it."

Evolutionist biology professor Lynn Margulis, in her book, <u>Acquiring Genomes: A Theory of the Origins of the Species</u> (p. 29), makes the same point: "Never, however, did

126

that one mutation make a wing, a fruit, a woody stem, or a claw appear....No evidence in the vast literature of heredity changes shows unambiguous evidence that random mutation itself, even with geographical isolation of populations, leads to speciation."

Neo-Darwinian evolution assumes (and requires) that micro changes from mutations (which are, in fact observable) resulted in advantageous *macro* changes in the past. Lee Spetner, Ph.D. Physics Professor at MIT, explains in his book Not by Chance (p. 160), "The neo-Darwinians would like us to believe that large evolutionary changes can result from a series of small events if there are enough of them. But if these events all lose information they can't be the steps in the kind of evolution the neo-Darwin theory is supposed to explain, no matter how many mutations there are. Whoever thinks macroevolution can be made by mutations that lose information is like the merchant who lost a little money on every sale but thought he could make it up on volume."

I.L. Cohen, mathematician and researcher, makes a similar point in his book, Darwin Was Wrong: A Study in Probabilities (p. 81): "To propose and argue that mutations even in tandem with 'natural selection' are the root-causes for 6,000,000 viable, enormously complex species, is to mock logic, deny the weight of evidence, and reject the fundamentals of mathematical probability."

Finally, Dr. John Sanford (PhD, Genetics), in Genetic Entropy & the Mystery of the Genome (pp. 26-27), states, "Bergman (2004) has studied the topic of beneficial mutations. Among other things, he did a simple literature

127

search via Biological Abstracts and Medline. He found 453,732 'mutation' hits, but among these only 186 mentioned the word 'beneficial' (about 4 in 10,000). When those 186 references were reviewed, almost all the presumed 'beneficial mutations' were only beneficial in a very narrow sense–but each mutation consistently involved loss of function changes—hence loss of information. While it is almost universally accepted that beneficial (information creating) mutations must occur, this belief seems to be based upon uncritical acceptance of RM [random mutation]/NS [natural selection], rather than upon any actual evidence. I do not doubt there are beneficial mutations as evidenced by rapid adaptation yet I contest the fact that they build meaningful information in the genome instead of degrade preexisting information in the genome."

Beneficial Mutations?

Are there any examples of beneficial mutations in any organism? The simple answer is "no," but academia strives to provide examples to the contrary.

One that is often suggested is sickle-cell anemia. This mutation can protect Native Africans from malaria. But does it provide an overall benefit to those who have it? The disease is a genetic disorder that changes the shape of red blood cells to a sickle shape rather than the normal disc shape. While it does protect the individual from malaria in high risk areas, sickle-shaped red blood cells carry less oxygen and tend to clump and get stuck in blood vessels. Sickle cells have a life expectancy of 10-20 days compared to healthy red blood cells that live 120 days. The body on average replaces red blood cells at the 120-day rate and isn't equipped to replace sickle cells that are dying more quickly than that. Thus the bodies of those affected are in a constant state of oxygen deprivation as well as periodic pain crises. The life expectancy for someone with sickle-cell anemia is only 42 years with the aid of modern medicine. This is an example of survival of the survivors, not survival of the fittest. If the whole population were to have this "beneficial mutation" the overall health of the human race would be much worse.

Another example of a beneficial mutation put forward by evolutionists is various bacteria, which can mutate to withstand certain antibiotics or survive on different food sources. However, the resulting mutant bacteria are weaker and have a shorter life expectancy. A closer examination of all the supposed "beneficial mutations" suggested within academia regarding bacteria show they either are not exclusively advantageous or the result of a built-in adaptation.

Evolutionary biologist Dr. Richard E. Lenski initiated a long-term experiment on February 24, 1988 that continues today. Its goal is to look for genetic changes in 12 initially identical populations of Escherichia coli bacteria that have been adapting to conditions in their flasks for more than 60,000 generations. The findings of the study so far? "Mutations that result in a gain of novel information have not been observed."

Neo-Darwinists have one answer they cling to for their theory, and that is "time." Time is their magic; anything can occur given enough time. However, we see that time is not a solution but instead a problem, as evolutionist

Dr. George Wald, (PhD, Zoology) from Columbia University, states in his book, <u>The Origin of Life: Physics and Chemistry of Life</u> (p. 12), "Time is in fact the hero of the plot...given so much time the 'impossible' becomes possible, the possible probable and the probable virtually certain. One has only to wait: time itself performs miracles. However, the laws of science suggest a problem with this idea. Those laws tell us very clearly that with time things degrade. They do not become better....Scientifically speaking then, time is the enemy of evolution, not its friend."

Genetic Entropy

Now that the entire human genome has been mapped, a massive effort is underway (through the Encyclopedia of DNA Elements, or ENCODE) to build a comprehensive "parts list" of all the functional elements. In 2012, a surprising finding came to light. Rather than DNA being composed mostly of useless "junk" (it had been thought that as much as 98% of genetic material could be classified this way), up to 80% of the human genome is, in fact, functional. That important discovery provides even more evidence of an intelligent designer and design.

We probably all have seen museum exhibits showing a life-size model of a chimpanzee-like creature that slowly changes into a human-like creature, then a modern human. This is meant to help "prove" that humans are directly evolved from animals. The genome tells a different tale. In 2012, geneticists Dr. Jeffrey Tomkins and Dr. Jerry Bergman reviewed the published studies comparing human and chimpanzee DNA. When the entire DNA is taken into account and not just pre-selected parts, they found, "it is safe to conclude that human-chimp genome similarity is not more than approximately 87% identical, and possibly not higher than 81%." Dr. Tomkins, in his own independent comparison, established the similarity to be around 70%. The evidence indicates we do not have ancestors in common with chimpanzees as we have been taught.

Another part of the genome study was called the 1000 Genome Project. An article in the American Journal of Human Genetics (Volume 91, Issue 6, pp. 1022–1032, 7 December 2012) reports that we all carry a large number of genetic mistakes and it is hard to find any that have benefited us at all. The investigation revealed that we are degrading, and not improving, as humans. The article also indicates the future looks grim for future generations of the human race, as we might not be able to handle many more generations of DNA deterioration.

Studying the human genome has uncovered even more evidence in conflict with Neo-Darwinian Evolution. Dr. John Sanford, in his book Genetic Entropy, and his videos available on YouTube, verifies that entropy (winding down) is evidenced in human DNA. As a PhD professor in Genetics, Sanford was a long time professor at Cornell University and during his career he believed and taught Neo-Darwinian evolution. Then over a ten-year period, he evolved from an atheist to a theistic evolutionist, and then a creationist who came to believe in the truth of the Bible and in Jesus Christ as his Savior.

After partially retiring from teaching, Sanford became interested in studying the results of the genome project. He discovered our DNA is adding mutations at a

131

rate much faster than evolution would assume. Evolutionists have long known that mutation rates of more than one mutation per generation would indicate genetic deterioration and the evolutionary theory would be impossible. The genome mapping project found that between 100 and 300 mutations were added in each generation. Sanford believes this information is known but guarded by population geneticists: "...humanity is degenerating at a rate as high as 1% every generation." He concludes we are in a downward spiral.

Evidence from the human genome project not only demonstrates that the human race is winding down, but also that we haven't been around that long. Alexey Kondrashov, (PhD, Biology) a professor at the University of Michigan, recognized the evidence of genetic entropy (Journal of Theoretical Biology, 175:583–594) and asked, "Why have we not died 100 times over?" He was puzzled since he believed humans have been on the earth for at least 100,000 years but the genetic evidence says this is impossible.

Dr. Sanford ends his book by asking two questions. First, if our genome did not actually arise via the accumulation of genetic "word-processing errors" (as is claimed), how *did* it come to be? Second, if our genomes are undergoing relentless degeneration - where can we possibly place our hope for the future?" He concludes, "I realized it had major implications for evolution, but I had no idea....I couldn't have guessed how profound the biblical implications are, how profoundly the evidence supports the biblical perspective of a dying universe and a dying world, we are dying because of the fall...and our only hope is Christ." We all have been infected with the disease of entropy and the human race is winding down, not progressing, as Darwinian Evolution claims.

On the same subject, Jacob A. Tennessen, PhD, an evolutionary geneticist at Oregon State University, in a Science article (Vol. 337, 6 July 2012, p. 67) entitled "Evolution and Functional Impact of Rare Coding Variation from Deep Sequencing of Human Exomes," concludes the degradation couldn't have been going on for a long period. He says, "The maximum likelihood time for accelerated growth was at a maximum 5,115 years ago." This short time period closely corresponds to the Biblical time of the Genesis flood, which began the period of genetic decline due to rapid growth of mutations. The mutation rate before the flood was most likely slower, due to less radiation and other more favorable environmental conditions. This is also evidenced by a much longer human life span during that period.

The Theory Fails

We have seen the evidence just does not match up with the mutations model or the overall model of evolution. Thomas Woodward, in a Moody magazine article entitled "Doubts about Darwin," quotes Colin Patterson, then senior paleontologist at the British Museum of Natural History in South Kensington, London: "For the last 18 months or so I've been kicking around non-evolutionary or even anti-evolutionary ideas. For over 20 years I had thought I was working on evolution in some way. One morning I woke up and something had happened in the night, and it struck me that I had been working on this stuff for more than 20 years, and there was not one thing I knew about it [to be true]. It's quite a shock to learn that one can be misled for so long. For the last few weeks I've tried putting a simple question to various people and groups: 'Can you tell me anything you know about evolution? Any one thing—that is true?'"

Lecturing to biologists at the American Museum of Natural History in New York City, Patterson said, "I tried that question on the geology staff at the Field Museum of Natural History and the only answer I got was silence. I tried it on the members of the Evolutionary Morphology Seminar in the University of Chicago, a very prestigious body of evolutionists, and all I got there was silence for a long time and eventually one person said, `I do know one thing—it ought not to be taught in high school.'" He continues, "I don't think we shall ever have any access to any form of [evolutionary] tree which we can call factual."

These are hard times for Darwinian evolution. Nobel Prize-winning physicist Robert B. Laughlin in his book, A Different Universe (pp. 168-169), states, "Much of present-day biological knowledge is ideological. A key symptom of ideological thinking is the explanation that has no implications and cannot be tested. I call such logical dead ends anti-theories because they have exactly the opposite effect of real theories: they stop thinking rather than stimulate it. Evolution by natural selection, for instance, which Charles Darwin originally conceived as a great theory, has lately come to function more as an anti-theory, called upon to cover up embarrassing experimental shortcomings and legitimize findings that are at best questionable."

On December 14, 2016 CNSnews.com reported on an article from macedoniaonline.eu, which covered the findings of a three-day meeting of the Royal Society. The article, "Scientists see the obvious, confirm Darwinism is broken," offers quotes from the meeting: "Darwinian theory is broken and may not be fixable. That was the takeaway from a meeting last month organized by the world's most distinguished and historic scientific organization, which went mostly unreported by the media..." And, "The neo-Darwinian mechanism of mutation and natural selection lacks the creative power to generate the novel anatomical traits and forms of life that have arisen during the history of life." They were looking for some new ideas that can explain how evolution could have happened, but none were found.

Does it matter?

But does this really matter? It does. F. Sherwood Taylor, British historian of science and a chemist who was director of the Science Museum in London, England, in his book Ideas and Beliefs of the Victorians (p. 195), says, "...I myself have little doubt that in England it was geology and the theory of evolution that changed us from a Christian to a pagan nation."

Atheist William B. Provine, Professor of Biological Science at Cornell University (in Origins Research 16(1), pp. 9 and 123) states, "...belief in modern evolution makes atheists of people. One can have a religious view that is compatible with evolution only if the religious view is indistinguishable from atheism....I agree a lot of people lose their faith after being taught Darwinian Evolution as fact and it disproves the Bible."

135

When evolution is taught as factual and proven science, Christians often turn away from the Christian faith, and others are prevented from trusting Jesus as their Savior. It is hard to understand why the truth, which seems obvious when deduced from the evidence, is so widely and avidly suppressed by lies.

Chapter Six

Worldviews in Conflict

"The best way to destroy your enemies is to make them
adopt your worldview."

- Bangambiki Habyarimana

"The quickest way to be deceived is to not think. If you turn
your brain off, someone else thinks for you."

-John Stonestreet

What is a worldview?

We all have different opinions and different
assumptions regarding what is true or right. How do we
reach such different conclusions about the same observed
realities? Our view of truth is determined by our worldview.
All of us develop our opinions of the world, our lives, our
culture, and every area of life either as God sees them or as
Satan wants us to see them. Worldview is an all-
encompassing topic. We all have developed a collection of
beliefs about life and how things should be, and we use these
assumptions to interpret every idea we encounter. Most of
us do not think through these assumptions, but either
accept or react to the beliefs to which we are exposed.

As theologian Francis Schaeffer puts it, "People
function on the basis of their worldview more consistently
than even they themselves may realize. The problem is not

outward things. The problem is having, and then acting upon, the right worldview—the worldview which gives men and women the truth of what is."

In this chapter we will assume there is a "right" worldview, a worldview based on the truth of the Bible. This statement will not be accepted by many today. However, when one has a Biblical worldview, based on correct assumptions, reality is seen for what it really is. It follows that a worldview based on wrong assumptions will distort one's interpretation of reality and lead to incorrect conclusions.

There are two basic worldviews; I will refer to the first as the "Biblical worldview" and to the opposite view as the "rebellious worldview." The rebellious worldview takes many forms—all of them contradictory to the Bible. Many Christians have accepted ideas from the rebellious worldview in some areas, such as theistic evolution. Those who tend to live by the rebellious worldview might accept some moral or Biblical principles, such as generosity to the poor. Few people are strictly on one side or the other but somewhere on the continuum from one extreme view to the other.

Assumptions of the Rebellious Worldviews

The rebellious worldview has many facets and forms, so I will try to describe some aspects to give you a better handle on this concept. Many with a rebellious worldview would deny the spiritual or supernatural. This viewpoint denies that God created the universe and posits that the material world is all there is. As astronomer and astrophysicist Carl Sagan has famously said, "The cosmos is all that is or was or ever will be."

Those who embrace the materialistic worldview believe everything in the universe can be explained in terms of natural phenomena, and they deny the possibility of any transcendent supernatural force or power beyond the universe, e.g., the God of the Bible. They reject God's order and instructions for living, as described in the Bible. They believe there is no such thing as objective truth, good, evil, or sin. The best they can come up with to explain evil in the world is to talk of a "balancing" of good and evil—similar to the good and bad side of the force in the Star Wars story. They may reject Biblical truths and distinctions made by God, including male and female, marriage and families, personal responsibility, and sovereign nations.

Philosophically, the rebellious worldview tends to assume that we all originated from the same source and we are all one. Unity becomes the highest goal. All our problems could be solved if we could all agree and become one again! This idea of all coming together as one stems from the ancient rebellious religions and philosophies. The Greek philosophers' primary goal was to achieve "unity in diversity" (from which we get the word university)—the desire that all (diverse) become one (unified). Unity sounds like a wonderful goal, until we see how it works out- unity under Sharia law or a communist dictator or even in a culture where any disagreement with what is deemed correct is not tolerated and instead ridiculed. Unity is also God's goal- but only unity with the truth at its center. And since God has given each person free will, this unity all mankind strives for will only be achieved through union with Jesus Christ.

Since the rebellious worldview denies a personal, supernatural Creator, some of its adherents believe that the power that created the universe is inside of them and they search for the answers to life by looking inward. Another tenet of the rebellious worldview is to elevate human reasoning to be the true source of progress. Personal feelings take preeminence over any objective truth and to the extent we follow our feelings or human emotional reasoning, society is evolving into a better future.

Many who embrace the rebellious worldview see science as the privileged form of knowledge. Science becomes the standard for evaluating truth and the basis for personal belief and faith. They maintain that science is about facts and truth, and might concede that religion could still have a role in inculcating values, such as honesty, charity, and morality. They see a problem, though, when Christians hold too tightly to the truth claims of the Bible and do not accept the truth claims of pseudo-science or other religions that are clearly contradictory to the Bible. The rebellious worldview sees those who hold to the Biblical worldview as the cause of problems in the world, and if they were removed things would be much better.

The rebellious worldview takes many forms and literally reaches into every area of life and academic study. One of its tenets is that it values feelings and individual subjective "truth" over reason and objective truth. As John Stonestreet of the Colson Center explains, "Everyone has a worldview, but most people do not think in terms of worldview. They don't connect what they say with the natural consequences if that played out just as they say. They will not let anyone tell them what is right or wrong. They have no absolutes of right and wrong, rather it is based on how they are feeling at the time. Every cultural expression communicates worldview ideas—i.e., movies, songs, TV, etc."

Assumptions of the Biblical Worldview

The Biblical worldview begins with the belief that God is the all-powerful and all-knowing Creator of everything in the universe, who created mankind and made the rules we are to live by, as explained in the Bible. Jesus Christ was the God/man who lived a sinless life and died on the cross to pay for our sins and then rose from the dead. Salvation is a free gift from God, received by grace through faith (belief) alone, and cannot be earned.

Jesus mandates a Biblical worldview in John 8:31-32: "So Jesus was saying to those Jews who had believed Him, 'If you continue in My word, then you are truly disciples of Mine; and you will know the truth, and the truth will make you free.'" Here Jesus is explaining that if we learn His thinking—the true worldview revealed in the Bible—we will be free. If someone has a rebellious worldview, it naturally follows that it will enslave them.

This worldview also holds to the unchanging moral truths inspired by God and written in the Bible. God has designed us in such a way that our lives will be better if we follow certain moral restrictions. However, many people reject God for this reason.

A fish in a fish bowl helps explain God's restrictions. Outside the bowl the fish would be free but have no life. True freedom is found in the fish bowl where the fish can thrive. God has given us the fish bowl of moral restrictions and we only will have true freedom in that bowl. Satan will offer "freedom" outside the bowl, but there the person is just flopping around, empty and not getting anywhere.

The Biblical worldview maintains that all Christians have the responsibility to share the hope of the gospel of Jesus Christ with other people, treat others in a manner reflecting that all people are created in God's image, live with personal virtue, obey the Biblical mandates, make disciples, and demonstrate love for all, being salt and light.

What does the Bible say about the Rebellious Worldview?

The original rebel was Lucifer, and he personifies the rebellious worldview. It was Lucifer's rebellious, prideful action that got him evicted from heaven. He was renamed "Satan," meaning "Adversary." One third of the angels rebelled against God alongside him, and he convinced Adam and Eve to rebel against God's rules as well.

Why do people fall for Satan's lies? His motivation was to be like God (Isaiah 14:14) and he didn't want to submit to God's authority and rules. He tempts humans in the same way, enticing them to be free from God's rules, to be like God, to be their own determiner of good and evil. He does this by convincing them to question and reject God and His Word.

God hates rebellion, as described in Isaiah 30:1: "Woe to the rebellious children," declares the LORD, "Who execute a plan, but not Mine, and make an alliance, but not of My Spirit, in order to add sin to sin." Often people start down this road because of a desire to do something that God has said is wrong. They put their desires and their feelings above God's commands, which is a dangerously easy first step. Eventually, to justify this choice or lifestyle, they reject God's word and God completely. All of us are either doing what is right in the eyes of God or doing what is right in our own eyes.

Psalm 14:1 and Psalm 53:1 both say, "The fool says in his heart, 'There is no God.'" The Hebrew word used for fool is *nabal* and the word does not imply a lack of intelligence but rather a lack of moral character. Thus, the verse could be translated as "The immoral person claims there is no God." Often a person will reject God's moral rules first and then reject the idea of a God Who has the right to determine morality and truth.

The apostle Paul describes the rebellious worldview in Romans 1:25: "...worshiped and served created things rather than the Creator." People either worship and serve the Creator God of the Bible (Biblical worldview) or elevate some aspect of the creation to worship (the rebellious worldview). This takes many forms, including worshiping the heavenly bodies, worshiping "Mother Earth," and the most common, elevating self above God.

Jesus tells us the devil is behind the rebellious worldview in John 8:44: "You belong to your father, the devil, and you want to carry out your father's desires. He was a murderer from the beginning, not holding to the truth, for there is no truth in him. When he lies, he speaks his native language, for he is a liar and the father of lies."

Paul ascribes the rebellious worldview to Satan in Ephesians 2:1-3: "As for you, you were dead in your transgressions and sins, in which you used to live when you followed the ways of this world and of the ruler of the kingdom of the air, the spirit who is now at work in those who are disobedient. All of us also lived among them at one time, gratifying the cravings of our flesh and following its desires and thoughts. Like the rest, we were by nature deserving of wrath."

Paul explains the rebellious worldview again in Romans 1:18-19: "For the wrath of God is revealed from heaven against all ungodliness and unrighteousness of men, who by their unrighteousness suppress the truth. For what can be known about God is plain to them, because God has shown it to them." Paul claims that every person knows there is a God, but many choose to suppress that knowledge of God and His righteous standards, and instead live as they choose. Once rules are removed, people may shock even themselves at how far away from God's values they drift.

2 Peter 2:18-19 tells us this rebellious worldview appeals to the lustful desires of the flesh, promising freedom, but instead enslaving its followers. The rebellious worldview has as its best attraction "freedom" from God's moral restrictions.

Christians are instructed to develop a Biblical worldview in Romans 12:2: "Do not conform to the pattern of this world, but be transformed by the renewing of your mind." Similarly, Colossians 2:8 says, "See to it that no one takes you captive through hollow and deceptive philosophy, which depends on human tradition and the elemental spiritual forces of this world rather than on Christ."

Next we will explore how one's worldview affects the way a person looks at various areas of life.

Looking at the Universe

A person's worldview colors the way they view all of nature. If they believe God created everything, they see miracles everywhere in nature. If they reject God as Creator, they see only the result of accidents, i.e., time plus chance.

Consider how Isaac Newton and Stephen Hawkins observe the same universe very differently. Newton, a Christian with a Biblical worldview, looked at the universe and came to this conclusion: "This most beautiful system of the sun, planets, and comets, could only proceed from the counsel and dominion of an intelligent and powerful Being....This Being governs all things, not as the soul of the world, but as Lord over all; and on account of his dominion he is wont to be called Lord God "pantokrator," or Universal Ruler..." (Newton, I., General Scholium)

But Stephen Hawkins, an atheist with a rebellious worldview, came to a different conclusion, as we see in his book, The Grand Design. He believes science has eclipsed, surpassed, and even killed philosophy. He uses flawed philosophy to state that the laws of physics and the law of gravity specifically are the only mechanism needed for the creation of the universe. "Because there is a law such as gravity, the universe can and will create itself from nothing. Spontaneous creation is the reason there is something rather than nothing, why the universe exists, why we exist. It is not necessary to invoke God to light the blue touchpaper and set the universe going."

Hawkins' worldview allows him to conveniently ignore how his ideas contradict observed reality and even common sense. He doesn't explain how the laws came to be in the first place or how the universe started by itself; his model is based on bad assumptions and bad philosophy.

Viewing Humans

The Biblical worldview states that humans are specially created in the image of God in order to have a relationship with God. Humans are superior to the rest of creation, uniquely possessing conscience, self-consciousness, rational thinking, emotional capacity, and a desire for relationships and meaning. Those with a Biblical worldview believe all creation belongs to God and He put us here as His caretakers and stewards of His created world. To put it simply: We came from God (creation); we turned away from God (the fall); God came to us (Jesus); now we can come to God (personal salvation); and God is coming back (the future reign of Christ over the entire universe). In God's design, His followers love all people as God has loved His Son, Jesus, and as Jesus has loved us.

The rebellious worldview suggests that humans and all living things are one; humans are nothing special in the universe. Historically, in rebellious cultures, human life is cheapened and expendable. Some with this worldview may

146

believe that man is born good and is not in need of a Savior. The problem with this is described by journalist Malcom Muggeridge: "The depravity of man is at once the most empirically verifiable reality but at the same time the most intellectually resisted fact."

The Bible teaches us that all people are created in God's image. God so loved the world that He sent His Son to veil His glory to come down to save us. Our identity is in how God sees all people as the objects of His love.

The rebellious worldview tells a person his or her sin pattern is actually their identity. The expression of those patterns (especially sexual sin patterns) is of the ultimate value and should never be suppressed. When a person sees his or her own identity to be rooted in their sexual identity, they feel all sexual urges should be acted on. They have a right to express that identity! The search for identity is really a search for meaning, yet in the end, sex does not fulfill the search for meaning.

There is a transcendence we all yearn for that is instilled in each of us by God since we are in His image, something that only a relationship with God can fulfill. As far back as Solomon, people have tried to fill this void with many things. In Ecclesiastes, Solomon describes how he tried human wisdom, wealth, work, relationships, sexual prowess, power, and all types of pleasure—yet all of these were empty and meaningless. He concludes in Ecclesiastes 12:13: "Now all has been heard; here is the conclusion of the matter: Fear God and keep His commandments, for this is the duty of all mankind."

Religions

The Biblical worldview believes there is one true religion, which is laid out in the Bible. Christianity is distinct from all other religions, in that God has come down in grace to save man from his hopeless sinful condition. In every other religion, the god is a harsh judge and mankind must keep on working to try to earn a way to heaven or a better afterlife.

The rebellious worldview takes many forms. Some versions are devoutly religious but with no assurance of eternal salvation. Others reject all established religious systems and see a unity of all religions as the true religion—their own form of rebellious one-ism.

Poet Steve Turner describes this worldview: "Jesus was a good man just like Buddha, Mohammed, and ourselves. We believe he was a good teacher of morals but we believe that his good morals are really bad. We believe that all religions are basically the same, at least the one we read was. They all believe in love and goodness, they only differ on matters of creation, sin, heaven, hell, God, and salvation." That sums it up pretty well.

According to theologian and Christian apologist William Lane Craig, "Unsophisticated religious pluralism responds to the religious diversity of mankind by saying, 'Well, they are all true! All of the world's religions are basically saying the same thing.' This view, which you very often find on the lips of college sophomores and laypeople, just evinces, frankly, tremendous ignorance of the teachings of the world's great religions. Anybody who has studied even a little bit of comparative religion knows that the worldviews that are propounded by these different religions are diametrically opposed to each other. Therefore, they cannot all be true."

What about Islam and Mormonism, for example? Islam has rejected the Bible, saying it has been corrupted. The worst sin in Islam is the belief that Jesus is God and that He died on the cross. Mormonism holds that Jesus was a brother of Satan and not the eternal God. Mormons also believe the Bible was corrupted. Both religions believe their new writings overrule the Bible. They allow for immoral things, such as multiple wives.

Looking at History and Government

Under the rebellious worldview, there is no purpose in history. As Henry Ford has said, "History is one damn thing after another." There is no meaning; all is random. The rebellious worldview encourages the culture to move away from the religious worldview because it has held us back in the past. Once we drop religious shackles, we can make progress in society and culture.

In the Biblical worldview, history is "His Story." God has made the world for His own pleasure and glory, and He has a purpose in history. God sees and knows everything— before human history and even into the future when the present heaven and earth will have passed away.

God controls history in three ways: direct control, by means of divine intervention; indirect control, through man's adherence to God's rules He has laid out; and permissive control, where God allows the free will of humans to run its course as long as it doesn't interfere with God's overall plan. God is sovereign and infinite, so He can use even terrible events in history to fulfill His purpose, which is to bring Him glory which He graciously shares with us.

With a Biblical worldview, God's hand can be seen throughout history. He has laid out certain rules and principles that man is to live by, and when they don't live by them bad things happen (this warning is given in Deuteronomy 28 and Leviticus 26). God often blesses a nation when its people follow His rules and plan. People see these blessings and notice the contrast, hopefully realizing the true God is the source and then coming to a saving knowledge of Jesus Christ. When a nation rebels, negative consequences follow, including economic problems, disease, and other calamities, which God may allow as a warning to repent. Eventually there will be invasions by outsiders and even enslavement.

Proverbs 29:2 warns, "When the righteous thrive, the people rejoice; when the wicked rule, the people groan." When a nation gives in to a rebellious worldview leader, the result is a heavy-handed totalitarian government. The state controls everything: the economy, the military, the laws, and religion. It opposes individual freedoms, such as civil rights, free speech, free enterprise, freedom of religion, freedom of assembly, and a free press. The leaders seek power, wealth, and control and will not accept anything that is sovereign over them, especially the God of the Bible. Their people become enslaved, and often the tyrant demands to be thought of as a deity.

The Bible tells us that during the years prior to the flood, the rebellious worldview filled the earth, resulting in corruption and violence. Genesis 6:5, 11, 12: "…and God saw that the wickedness of man was great in the earth, and that every imagination of the thoughts of his heart was only evil continually. The earth was corrupt before God and the earth was filled with violence." Corruption and violence are symptoms of a rebellious worldview. The Old Testament is full of examples of the nations of Israel and Judah obeying God's laws and prospering, or doing what is right in their own eyes (disobeying God) with disastrous consequences for the nation.

These principles were well established by the Scriptures and are still in place today. Here is one historical example. The French revolution of 1789 started with the promise of "Liberty, Equality and Fraternity." This was an atheistic revolt that originated with the ideas of Voltaire and his written attacks on the Bible in the previous generation. The people were lured with the promise of freedom from the moral restraints of the Bible. Once the revolt took hold in France, it led to a reign of enslavement, terror, and death. More than 375,000 were killed. The revolutionists were clearly rebellious as they closed churches, forbade crosses, destroyed religious monuments, outlawed public and private worship and religious education. Amidst the domestic instability and social confusion, Napoleon began his rise toward dictatorship.

The rebellious worldview received an important validation from Charles Darwin in Origins. Darwinian evolution as part of the rebellious worldview is validated by

Christian apologist Greg Koukl: "If Darwinism is true, then there is no purpose or meaning to life, there is no morality, there's no qualitative difference between humans and animals, there's no life after death, and there's no purpose to human history. Now, are you trying to tell me that it doesn't really matter if people believe we evolved or not?"

Darwin promised freedom from Biblical morality, just as the French Revolution did. Novelist and philosopher Aldous Huxley admits this in his book, Ends and Means. "I had motives for not wanting the world to have a meaning; and consequently assumed that it had none....The philosophy of meaninglessness was essentially an instrument of liberation from a certain system of morality. We objected to the morality because it interfered with our sexual freedom."

Darwin, writing in his earliest speculations on the origin of man, expressed concern that the philosophical (worldview) ramifications of his conclusions could be dire. He knew the possibility of how "nature red in tooth and claw" could engender horrific carnage in the years, decades, and centuries to come.

Philosopher Fredrick Nietzsche followed Darwinism to its logical conclusion that "God is dead." He believed atheists of the twentieth century would realize that the Biblical morals they had been living by were outdated and people would create their own moral standard. Because of this, Nietzsche prophesied the twentieth century would be the "bloodiest century in human history." He turned out to be quite right.

Many twentieth century revolutions were justified based on Darwinian evolutionary theory...with deadly results. This quote from Theodore Robert Beale, professionally known as Vox Day, sums up the century: "There have been 28 countries in world history that have been ruled by regimes with avowed atheists at the helm. The total body count for the 90 years between 1917 and 2007 is approximately 148 million deaths at the bloody hands of 52 atheists, three times more than all the human beings killed by war, civil war and individual crime in the entire twentieth century combined."

Hitler fooled the Christians in Germany in order to take power under his rebellious worldview. The total number of noncombatants killed by the Germans was around 11 million.

Nietzsche was correct about the twentieth century being the bloodiest in the history of man, once the morality of God was abandoned. The rebellious worldview is a philosophy of death. Proverbs 14:12: "There is a way that appears to be right, but in the end it leads to death."

Moving Towards a More Biblical Worldview

Some revolutions in recent history moved nations toward a more Biblical worldview, and each resulted in more freedom for their people. 2 Corinthians 3:17: "Now the Lord is the Spirit, and where the Spirit of the Lord is, there is freedom." The first was in England and was known as the "Glorious Revolution," the Revolution of 1688, or the "Bloodless Revolution." This led to freedom for the citizens based on a move to a more Biblical worldview.

Next was the American Revolution (1775–1783), also known as the War for Independence. In England King George III and others thought of the revolution as the "Presbyterian rebellion" as they recognized that Protestant ministers were the driving force behind the revolt, acknowledging that it clearly was a move towards a Biblical worldview.

I believe the U.S. Constitution is the most Biblically inspired secular government document in the history of mankind. As John Adams (a Christian) wrote to Thomas Jefferson on June 28, 1813: "The general principles on which the fathers achieved independence were the general principles of a Biblical perspective. I will avow that I then believed, and now believe, that those general principles of Christianity are as eternal and immutable as the existence and attributes of God."

Governeur Morris, another signer of the Constitution and the author of its Preamble, understood the importance of a Biblical worldview in avoiding tyranny: "For avoiding the extremes of despotism or anarchy...the only ground of hope must be on the morals of the people. I believe that religion is the only solid base of morals and that morals are the only possible support of free governments. Therefore education should teach the precepts of religion and the duties of man towards God."

Worldview in the United States Today

The United States clearly is moving toward a rebellious worldview and we can expect to see an increase in violence, a loss of freedom, and an increase in tyranny in our future. Conservative talk show host Dennis Prager sums up what is happening in our country today: "With the demise of the biblical religions that have provided the American people with their core values since their country's inception, we are reverting to the pagan worldview. Trees and animals are venerated, while man is simply one more animal in the ecosystem—and largely a hindrance, not an asset."

When the people get out of control you can expect a much stronger police presence in the country, as validated by Robert Winthrop, Speaker of the U. S. House of Representatives more than 100 years ago: "Men, in a word, must necessarily be controlled either by a power within them or by a power without them; either by the Word of God or by the strong arm of man; either by the Bible or by the bayonet."

One of our Founding Fathers, Samuel Adams, confirms that thought: "A general Dissolution of Principles & Manners will more surely overthrow the Liberties of America than the whole Force of the Common Enemy. While the People are virtuous they cannot be subdued; but when once they lose their Virtue they will be ready to surrender their Liberties to the first external or internal Invader." When the rebellious worldview takes power in the government, it becomes not the servant but the master of the people. The people have good reason to fear the government, and they become enslaved.

The prophets of old were spokesmen, warning the people and the government when they were on a rebellious path. Speaking out will usually be met with criticism, but

God has given us His word and His thinking in order to reach out to the world for Him.

In 1790, Irish statesman Edmund Burke wrote his classic essay, "Reflections on the Revolution in France" in which he explains why the French Revolution would end badly. He was strongly criticized, as his view was not politically correct, but Burke had the proper Biblical worldview and saw the revolution was a rebellious movement. He bravely prophesied the coming terror and tyranny. He was proved right, but it was too late for many.

What must we do?

God is looking for men and women who dare to speak out. In this chapter I provided a brief introduction to the conflicting worldviews. There are many more areas of life where rebellion has infiltrated into the prevailing cultural opinions. Often these strongly held opinions are "felt" rather than based on reason and thought.

There is virtually no area of life where the Bible does not provide guidance for truthful viewpoints. We have covered only a few topics here. Hopefully this introduction sets the groundwork for a better understanding of the competing worldviews to allow readers to evaluate the ideas that confront them every day.

Christians are called to contend for the faith, to make the case for the Biblical worldview to the world. Burke also famously said: "The only thing necessary for the triumph of evil is for good men to do nothing."

156

An inaccurate worldview hinders the gospel, according to Ronald H. Nash, long time philosophy professor at Reformed Theological Seminary: "The reason some people reject Christianity is not due to their problems with one or two isolated Christian beliefs; their dissent results rather from the fact that their fundamentally anti-Christian worldview leads them to reject information and arguments that support the Christian worldview."

I encourage you to study the Bible to become immersed in God's thinking. If you are interested in learning more about worldview, tremendous resources are available. One is Dr. Peter Jones' website, truthxchange.com. There is a short online course there, including articles and videos. Or read Dr. Peter Jones' book, One or Two: Seeing a World of Difference and other books.

Additionally, check out the Colson Center for Christian Worldview. Summit Ministries is another valuable resource. I also encourage you to study the works of Francis Schaeffer, a well-spoken evangelical Christian theologian, and Nancy Pearcey, a noted evangelical author.

Once you see the world with the proper worldview, I encourage you to make a difference. Speak out and defend the Biblical worldview and proclaim the Creator God of the Bible.

Chapter Seven

The Problem of Evil and Suffering in the World

"The fact of suffering undoubtedly constitutes the single greatest challenge to the Christian faith, and has been in every generation. Its distribution and degree appear to be entirely random and therefore unfair. Sensitive spirits ask if it can possibly be reconciled with God's justice and love."

-John Stott, theologian

The existence of evil and suffering leads many Christians to question God's love, His power, or even His existence. It can prevent some people from believing in a loving God or coming to faith in Jesus. Charles Darwin was said to have rejected Christianity after suffering the death of his daughter. A recent biography stated, "Annie's cruel death destroyed Charles's tatters of belief in a moral, just universe. Later he would say that this period chimed the final death-knell for his Christianity."

How should Christians understand evil and suffering? Is God still alive? Does He care about our suffering? Can He stop evil or is He powerless? After all, if we were the all-powerful God, wouldn't we rid the world of everything evil and all suffering? Why doesn't God just make everything right, if He really can?

We will examine evil and suffering from God's perspective in this chapter. Romans 11:33-34 says, "Oh, the depth of the riches both of the wisdom and the knowledge of God! How unsearchable are His judgments and unfathomable His ways! For who has known the mind of the Lord, or who has become His counselor?"

The presence of sin and evil, and its resultant suffering in the world, is an intellectual problem that must be resolved if we are to see God as He is. Yet even more, it is the root of many doubts, or at least the excuse for the doubters. On a personal level, we cry out to God, "*Why?*" when suffering comes to us. Even believers become angry at God or turn their backs on Him when terrible things happen. We will look at this issue both intellectually and personally.

Often we forget (or deny) one thing: that we have evil in us! I John 1:8: "If we say that we have no sin, we deceive ourselves, and the truth is not in us." Romans 3:23: "For all have sinned and fall short of the glory of God." So if we are going to eliminate sin and evil in the world, we have to rid God's world of all people, ourselves included.

We know from Genesis 1 and 2 that God created a perfect world and perfect mankind. So after that did God create evil? No, God is never the creator of evil. Evil entered the world when Adam and Eve disobeyed God the first time. But couldn't God have stopped them? Of course He could have, but instead He gave them (and us) free will to choose for or against Him. He doesn't force Himself on us.

What is Evil?

Suppose someone tells you:
1) God is the creator of everything that exists.
2) Evil exists.
3) Therefore, God is the creator of evil.

This would be a logical conclusion *if* evil is a "thing"—that is, if it is part of everything. However, in the Biblical view, evil is not really a thing in itself, but the absence of or perversion of "good." Christian philosopher J. P. Moreland states, "Evil is a lack of goodness. It is goodness spoiled. You can have good without evil, but you cannot have evil without good." Just as cold is the absence of heat and darkness is the absence of light, so evil is the absence of good.

Evil is anything that contradicts or violates the holy nature of God. God is the ultimate good. Evil is the result of creatures' rejection of that good and turning to rebellious choices and actions. God did not make it impossible for evil to exist because He did not make it impossible for mankind to reject Him.

When God created the world, He designed it in an exact way for mankind to prosper. It was described as "very good." (Genesis 1:31) Then He created mankind, the only creature with the capability to share His love, His glory, and His fellowship. God the Father, God the Son, and God the Holy Spirit always had perfect love and perfect coexistence in relationship. Then they said, in Genesis 1:26a, "Let us make man in our own image, in our likeness..." God loved us from the beginning, and His desire is that we know Him and love Him fully, without any coercion—by our own free choice.

So who is the first author of evil? The devil, also called Satan, the original rejecter of the good, has been sinning from the beginning. (I John 3:8)

In Ezekiel 28:11-17 and Isaiah 14:12-14 we get a glimpse of a time before the creation of our world, when God created the angels. Satan was created by God as a beautiful angel of light. He was blameless in all he did until the day evil was found in him. This is the day he said, "I will be like the Most High."

Satan persuaded one third of God's created angels to rebel with him, and there has been an invisible warfare between the fallen and the holy angelic creatures ever since. Satan is "the ruler of the kingdom of the air, the spirit who is now at work in those who are disobedient." (Ephesians 2:2) Most of us are unaware of this invisible warfare, but the angels of God are watching and rejoice when one sinner repents (Luke 15:10).

Evil does not disprove the existence of a loving God, but evil can prove Satan is alive and active. Satan wants us to believe God does not love us, or even exist.

Alternative Worldviews of Evil and Suffering

How do other worldviews make sense of evil? The problem of evil and suffering is not unique to the Christian community; every culture or worldview must address this issue. But outside the Biblical worldview, there are no reasonable explanations.

Atheist philosopher Friedrich Nietzsche argued that "evil is a problem we brought on ourselves, by inventing

162

moral categories that don't reflect the ways of the natural world." In other words, if there was nothing we considered good, there would be no evil. He is right—in the natural world there should not be evil, but there is. Without "good" defined, we can't call anything evil, because who is qualified to make those distinctions? If everything evolved randomly, no one can say what is good or not good; it just *is*. All things are the result of morally neutral random events.

Worldviews influenced by Eastern pantheism consider evil and suffering as merely illusions created by the human mind—they are not real. Thus there is no attempt to make things better, since the suffering is an illusion. Perhaps in the next life circumstances will be better.

Without a true standard, classifying something as "evil" is a subjective exercise, based on cultural beliefs. After all, some cultures condone murder and child sacrifice. Without an absolute good, no one can say something is evil without basing it on their own feelings and experience.

When challenged about the existence of evil by an unbeliever, ask how they define "good" and "evil." Unless there is an absolute good, how can something be designated as evil? If everything is the result of random mutations over millions and millions of years, who decides what is right and wrong? And for that matter, why hasn't evil evolved away by now?

Helen Keller suffered from blindness and deafness her entire life. Yet she became a believer in Jesus Christ and thanked God for her handicaps, for "through them, I have found myself, my work, and my God."

163

She provides additional insight into how the various worldviews see suffering. "The Jewish and Christian Bible view of handicapped persons is strikingly different from other belief systems. The traditional Islamic attitude is that a handicapped person is being punished or cursed of Allah. 'Such are the men whom Allah has cursed for he has made them deaf and blinded their sight'. (Quran 47:23) The Hindu and Buddhist attitude is that a handicapped person is being punished for sins of a supposed past life by an impersonal 'bad' karma. The Socialist [or humanistic evolutionary] attitude is that a handicapped person is a burden on the State, being worth less because of their limited capacity to contribute to society. The Jewish attitude is in Leviticus 19:14: 'Do not curse the deaf or put a stumbling block in front of the blind, but fear your God. I am the Lord.' Also Deuteronomy 27:18: 'Cursed is anyone who leads the blind astray on the road.' The Christian attitude was expressed by Jesus, Who said (Matthew 25:40), 'Truly I tell you, whatever you did for the least of these brothers and sisters of mine, you did for me.'"

Free Will and Evil

Love and devotion not freely offered are not really love. If there is such a thing as a free choice to obey and love God, then there must be such a thing as a free choice to disobey God and reject Him. Rejection of God, resulting in separation from God, is the origin of evil and suffering. As University of Notre Dame Professor Alvin Plantinga explains, "To create creatures capable of moral good, therefore, He must create creatures capable of moral evil; and He can't give these creatures the freedom to perform evil and at the same time prevent them from doing so. The fact that free creatures sometimes go wrong, counts neither against God's omnipotence nor against His goodness."

Christian apologist Dr. Norman Geisler, in his book Chosen but Free, points out: "Reason also demands that all moral creatures are morally free, that is, they have the ability to respond one way or another. Whatever evil we do and are responsible for, we could have responded otherwise."

God's Wide View

Consider world history from God's perspective, at least that portion He has revealed to us. God created everything in perfection—it was "very good," as we have seen. There was no sin, no evil, and no death. God created the finely tuned universe. He created a man and a woman in His image, capable of a loving relationship with Himself. He walked with them in the cool of the day. (Genesis 3:8)

God laid down one rule for His creation, a prohibition designed to protect mankind and keep them in perfect relationship with their Creator. It is found in Genesis 2:16-17: "And the Lord God commanded the man, 'You are free to eat from any tree in the garden; but you must not eat from the tree of the knowledge of good and evil, for when you eat from it, you will certainly die." The consequences were clear; they had a choice. Yet Adam and Eve chose to disobey God and ate the fruit.

They followed Satan in rebelling against God, in thinking they knew better than God. This introduced sin (the knowledge of good and evil) and a curse on the whole creation, as we are told in Genesis 3:17: "Because you listened to your wife and ate fruit from the tree about which I commanded you, 'You must not eat from it'...Cursed is the ground because of you."

This curse is further explained in Romans 8:22: "We know that the whole creation has been groaning as in the pains of childbirth right up to the present time." This was the result of Adam's sin, as we find in Romans 5:12: "Therefore, just as sin entered the world through one man, and death through sin, and in this way death came to all people, because all have sinned." Sin and death have spread throughout all of God's creation.

In human history, we are now in what has been called the "messy middle." We are not in the perfection of the Garden of Eden, but rather in the time after Adam's fall. We joyfully anticipate the future, when Jesus Christ will return to restore all things in heaven and on earth to the perfect state they were at creation, and to rule in perfect justice and righteousness. He has promised this, and His second coming is just as sure as His first coming that occurred over 2,000 years ago. However, now, in this period of time between the two perfect ages, each person is born separated from the perfect fellowship with God that God so desired when He created mankind. Our lives are full of struggles, disobedience, greed, shame, and self-centeredness. We suffer just because that is how the world is, and we suffer because of the evil and sinful decisions of ourselves and others.

To understand God, and how God views sin, we need to think of Him the way He is actually revealed in the Bible. God is not just a better version of us. God is totally above and beyond us. We do not think like God. Life is sacred to God, and it should be to us. We are not the masters of the universe; we are the rebels against God's perfect design and creation. Because of God's perfection, He *must* judge sin and He cannot be associated with it. We are powerless to overcome this barrier on our own.

But even though we have abandoned God, He did not abandon us. Right after the fall, when the effects of the curse of disobedience were revealed, God first promised His ultimate solution: The One Who would crush Satan's head.

The entire Old and New Testaments of the Bible reveal His gracious provision for us and what he desires for us, and they reveal glimpses of His glory. He knew His Son, Jesus Christ, was the only One qualified to become the God-man, to humble Himself, to veil His glory, and to suffer and die.

God started solving the problem of sin and evil by sending His Son, Jesus Christ, to the cross. Jesus suffered the consequences of sin mentioned in Genesis 3, namely the shame of nakedness and the thorns that represented the curse on creation. Jesus was naked and wore a crown of thorns on the cross. He bore the wrath of the judgment of God due to each of us. He paid the ransom price to redeem sinful people and the whole creation. Only His sacrifice, as sinless humanity, voluntarily suffering our punishment, could satisfy the perfect righteousness and justice of God. When we trust Him as our Savior, the way is open to intimate, though still invisible, fellowship with God, even while we are on this sinful earth. God always knew we would sin, and He provided the solution to make things right. Still, God is a Gentleman—He will never coerce us to accept the free gift of the sacrifice of Jesus Christ. If we choose to leave the Gift unopened and unaccepted, we are, in effect, depending on ourselves to work out our own eternal salvation, which of course is impossible.

Even now, during the messy middle, when we live in the worst of times, after the perfection of the first garden and before the return of Jesus Christ in perfect rule over heaven and earth, we still have the possibility of joy in the midst of suffering. God knows all the knowable, even all the possible. His wisdom is infinite and He can use even evil things and work them out for good. His "good" is our close walk and dependence on Him, not necessarily our comfortable circumstances.

Professor Plantinga writes: "As the Christian sees things, God does not stand idly by, coolly observing the suffering of His creatures. He enters into and shares our suffering. He endures the anguish of seeing his son, the second person of the Trinity, consigned to the bitterly cruel and shameful death of the cross. Christ was prepared to endure the agonies of hell itself...in order to overcome sin, and death, and the evils that afflict our world, and to confer on us a life more glorious than we can imagine. He was prepared to suffer on our behalf, to accept suffering of which we can form no conception."

Finally, He will take those who have put their faith in Him to a place without sin forever. Revelation 21:4: "And God shall wipe away all tears from their eyes; and there shall be no more death, neither sorrow, nor crying, neither shall there be any more pain: for the former things are passed away." Eternity is a long time. In the perfect eternal state, even the worst earthly suffering will seem like nothing. As Paul said in 2 Corinthians 4:17: "For our light and momentary troubles are achieving for us an eternal glory that far outweighs them all." Troubles may last a lifetime, but that is still a drop in the ocean of all eternity in perfection.

Some may say evil is an argument against God, but ironically it is God who is the only solution to the problem of suffering and evil. The Bible warns that those who reject Christ will taste a "second death," an eternal separation from God. Revelation 21:8: "They will be consigned to the fiery lake of burning sulfur. This is the second death." This is only right; for those who choose to be separated from God, God will grant them their wish...for all eternity.

Is There any Purpose for Evil in the World?

Wouldn't life be better without sin and evil and suffering and pain? I once knew of a child who had a rare condition—she was unable to feel pain. This child could be sick or seriously injured and never know it. Her parents had to be constantly vigilant! While it sounds good to not have pain, pain is an indicator that we have a problem.

In the same way, the presence of evil in the world should point us to the One who is good. Evil and suffering make us aware we have a problem—that we are separated from God. God provides the only solution.

Christian apologist C.S. Lewis, no stranger to suffering, wrote The Problem of Pain (1940) in which he suggests that people have lost the sense of the seriousness of sin, and God can use suffering as a reminder of this horror. We minimize our sin, but it cost God a lot. Our world is not good; we live in a world cursed as a judgment on sin. Lewis points out: "God whispers to us in our pleasures, speaks in our conscience, but shouts in our pains: it is his megaphone to rouse a deaf world."

The death and suffering that are part of this life are powerful reminders that something is wrong with creation and with humanity. Suffering and evil are the consequences of sin as well as a reminder that He will judge us in the future. God intends for this to point people to the solution—Jesus Christ, God's ultimate answer to the problem of evil and our way to avoid future judgment.

Hebrews 9:27 tells us, "Just as people are destined to die once, and after that to face judgment." For those who haven't trusted in Jesus as Savior, there is a reason to fear God; they will be eternally judged for their sins. But those who have trusted in Christ as their Savior have no reason to fear. John 3:36: "Whoever believes in the Son has eternal life, but whoever rejects the Son will not see life, for God's wrath remains on them."

Often, in a time of suffering, such as war or famine or natural disaster, people who have never considered or needed God will be faced with their own powerlessness over their circumstances, and begin to seek the security that comes from knowing God.

We do not know God's mind; we are not His counsellors. As the Creator of all things He has no obligation to explain Himself to us. We do not know why every bad

170

thing happens, but we do know the God Who is in control, and He is good. He is sovereign. He can cause all things to work together for the good of those who love Him (Romans 8:28). During the messy middle, God still offers mankind a chance to turn to Him. He hasn't yet put an end to evil and suffering in the world, but we know He will in the future.

The Problem of Death

Solved by resurrection! Death is to be feared if we don't know for sure what will happen to us when we die. Death is a transition, but for the believer in Jesus Christ, it is a glorious one. Because of the worst death, the greatest evil in history, the death of Jesus on the cross and His victorious ressurection, the best of all things are available to us in heaven. Christians do not have to fear death.

Jesus promises us in John 14:19, "Before long, the world will not see me anymore, but you will see me. Because I live, you also will live." Psalm 116:15: "Precious in the sight of the Lord is the death of his saints." Death is "precious" because sinners who have trusted Christ will enter immediately into the presence of their Creator. 2 Corinthians 5:8: "...absent from the body, present with the Lord..." Glory is described in 1 Corinthians 2:9 as, "What no eye has seen, what no ear has heard, and what no human mind has conceived—the things God has prepared for those who love him." Paul understood this in Philippians 1:21 when he said, "For to me, to live is Christ and to die is gain."

The timing, the means, the place, and the circumstances of the death of our earthly body all depend on our sovereign God. We can trust Him; He has us here for a reason and He will take us home at the perfect time.

Suffering is Expected in the Christian Life!

So, once you believe in Jesus Christ as your Savior, is that the end of your suffering? Not at all, not during the messy middle anyway. Believers still have their old sin nature so they still commit personal sins. Jesus died for these sins and so as His children, believers will never pay the eternal penalty. However, these sins build a separation between a believer and God, until in humility the believer confesses them to Him and regains the fellowship He wants us to have with him. So even as a Christian you may suffer as God tries to get your attention, as a parent would with a child.

Even while walking in fellowship with your Savior, you will suffer because you are a believer in Jesus Christ. While the believer has gained a loving Friend and has available the very power that raised Jesus Christ from the dead in the indwelling Holy Spirit, he or she has also gained an enemy—Satan and his fallen angels. Once you have believed in Jesus Christ, opposition to your witness arises from these invisible forces. The world we live in often opposes and persecutes the things of God as well. The people of the world do not want to be accountable to the righteous God and they may resent you as His representative on earth. John 15:18-19: "If the world hates you, keep in mind that it hated Me first. If you belonged to the world, it would love you as its own. As it is, you do not belong to the world, but I have chosen you out of the world. That is why the world hates you."

Hebrews 10:32-34 speaks to believers about this: "Remember those earlier days after you had received the light, when you endured in a great conflict full of suffering. Sometimes you were publicly exposed to insult and persecution; at other times you stood side by side with those so treated. You suffered along with those in prison, and joyfully accepted the confiscation of your property, because you knew that you yourselves had better and lasting possessions." There is comfort and a promise for the suffering Christian in Romans 8:17: "...if indeed we suffer with Him so that we also may be glorified with Him." This implies the rewards for all eternity that belong to the Christian who endures faithfully through suffering while on the earth.

Evil and suffering affect every person in this world. But for believers in Jesus Christ, God provides the resources and the truth so we can live a life of eternal significance and glorify God in a fallen world. He has not left us alone; He understands and has suffered more than we ever will.

Examples of Suffering in the Bible

Before we try to see our suffering as God sees it, let us get a glimpse into His mind by looking at a few examples of suffering from the Bible. God reveals His character as He deals with real people, their sin and suffering, and the consequences of their choices. He is perfectly loving, but also perfectly just. Sometimes, when people or groups are rebelling against Him, He must punish some in order to preserve the freedom to accept or reject His offer of salvation for others.

In the Biblical narrative, it is hard to find someone who did not suffer. There are many more examples than those we will present here. Through these stories, we will see that some suffering is self-inflicted; in other cases, it comes as the result of circumstances out of our control or because of bad decisions of others. Sometimes the suffering is designed to demonstrate the glory of God in how He delivers through it or uses it for His purpose. In other cases, we may never know the reason for it.

When we observe suffering as a result of God's judgment, we must remember that God is perfectly just, perfectly sovereign, the Creator of everything, and its determiner. When He judges, it is the result of our sin. He hates sin, and knows much better than we do how deserving of judgment it is.

In the time of Noah, God observed the corruption and violence of the human race. Genesis 6:5: "The Lord saw how great the wickedness of the human race had become on the earth, and that every inclination of the thoughts of the human heart was only evil all the time."

Through their freely taken actions, the survival of the human race was threatened by evil out of control. Yet God saw and saved Noah, a righteous man, and his family. In a foreshadowing of the future deliverance available to all people through the cross, God directed Noah to build a large ark to save him and his family, as well as many of God's other creatures. Men were to be stewards of God's creation, but their violence and evil was destroying it. God stepped in to save the human race from itself.

In the example of Joseph in Genesis chapters 37, 39-47, and 50, we see a man who suffered not directly because of his own sin or evil, but because of his brothers' evil decision to sell him into slavery. Yet we also see God use Joseph during and through that time of suffering—his life was preserved and he even prospered. He was God's instrument to save the lives of all his family and the land of Egypt during a time of great famine. God did not cause Joseph's brothers to betray him, but our infinite God is able to use evil circumstances to bring about good, in this case the preservation of many lives. During those twenty years in slavery and prison, Joseph had no idea why he was suffering. Yet looking back, he can see God's hand as he tells his brothers in Genesis 50:20, "You intended to harm me, but God intended it for good to accomplish what is now being done, the saving of many lives."

What about the Israelites' invasion and conquest of Canaan? Genesis 15:16 tells us that even though God had promised Abraham's descendants the land, He did not allow Israel to enter it or to conquer the Canaanites (Amorites) until the sin of the Amorites had reached its full measure.

As the Creator of the human race, God imposes rules designed to preserve freedom. All people are free to decide if they want to obey and rightly relate to Him or not. Sins that degrade and destroy humanity, like perverted sexual practices, human sacrifice, and pagan idol worship cannot be allowed by God to continue. Only God decides when He has extended enough time to give rebellious people a chance to repent and turn in obedience to His mercy.

God values His own creation—even the very land. In Leviticus 18:24-28 we see the Canaanites have so defiled the land with their sins that the land will "vomit" them out. God instructs the Israelites to destroy them, but also tells Israel they, too, could be vomited out of the land if they defile it with *their* disobedience. Always there is grace extended—as long as any foreigners live with Israel in obedience to God they will be safe. God reserves the sovereign right to preserve His creation by destroying those who rebel against Him. God is patient to give grace to turn from disobedience; those who obey are preserved. The account of the destruction of Sodom and Gomorrah demonstrates this as well. Lot and his family were preserved—they were the only righteous persons found in those cities.

David suffered tremendously under Saul, who was pursuing David, and continually plotting to kill him for many years. David had done nothing to deserve this, so why would God allow it? We cannot know the mind of God, but by reading some of the Psalms we can understand what God was doing within David at this time. God was building a trust in David that would be necessary when he became king. David was learning to depend on God for His very life. David became a man after God's own heart, who would do everything God wanted him to do (Acts 13:22). David was inspired to write Psalms 7, 34, 52, 54, 56, 57, 59, 142, and others in which he pleads to God for protection and reminds Him of his problems and his enemies. Then, as he remembers Who God is and how He has preserved and blessed him, David praises Him for His faithfulness, strength, and love. He goes from hopelessness to praise—a wonderful example and reminder for us! Innumerable suffering Christians have found hope in these words from God written through David's suffering.

David suffered considerably after he seduced Bathsheba and had her husband Uriah killed (2 Samuel 11-13). This suffering resulted from David's own sin. He repented and turned back to God, but the consequences remained. The child of Bathsheba from the adulterous relationship died. Yet even here we see the grace of God. For those who have lost a child, I can imagine no worse pain. But in 1 Samuel 12:23, David understands: "I will go to him one day, but he cannot return to me." David realized he was living in the messy middle where suffering exists, but for all of eternity he would be with his son.

When babies and young children die, they go directly to heaven into the love of their heavenly Father. Remember this when you see children dying from the evil in this world—from famine, abuse, war, and other horrible circumstances—God loves each of them more than we are capable of loving, and does not hold them accountable when they are too young to understand their need for salvation. They are immediately in heaven, where there are no more tears, no more sorrow, and no more pain.

Very few can top Job's level of suffering. Job never knew why he suffered, but we are offered an inside look into the conflict and witness of heaven. Satan had been observing Job, a blameless and upright man who feared God and shunned evil. (Job 1:8) Satan was confident Job only loved God because of the way God had blessed him. God then allowed Satan to take away every one of those blessings—his wealth, his children, his possessions, and even his

177

health. Again, Job had no idea why all this was happening and his friends did not understand either.

Job questions God in the book of Job chapters 23-24, but God never tells Job why this is happening. He never reveals that all of heaven is observing whether or not Job will deny God. Job knows he is innocent, but that for some reason he has been singled out for suffering. But *why* is not the issue. Instead, God tells Job *Who* He is! (Job 38-41) He is the sovereign Creator and Sustainer of everything in the world. Job 41:11: "Who has a claim against Me that I must pay? Everything under heaven belongs to Me."

God was gracious to give Job a beautiful picture of Himself. This perspective of God was the key for Job enduring his situation. Once he understands Who God is— the Creator of everything and the only One Who can sustain it all—Job can only fall down and worship! Job says, "My ears had heard of you, but now my eyes have seen you. Therefore I despise myself and repent in dust and ashes." (Job 42:5-6)

We often think of ourselves as just a little lower than God, and maybe almost as wise. Job got the real picture! The Creator is everything; the clay is nothing. Our ability to understand all the ways of God is infinitely less likely than a newborn being able to understand an adult conversation.

God repeatedly warned Israel and Judah not to worship anything or anyone but Him. He was their God, and there was no other. He gave Moses the rules they were to live by. All He wanted was for His people to love and worship Him above anything else. What less could their

Creator and the One Who provided for all their needs expect? But as they continually rebelled and occasionally temporarily repented, God said, enough. He had warned them. He sent many prophets and issued many warnings. Still the people continually returned to their idol worship.

Finally, God sent Israel and Judah into captivity after at least 700 years of their rebellion and His warnings. This is not something God enjoyed doing—He describes Israel as His unfaithful wife whom He will take back at any time, but still she remains unfaithful. There was a limit to their exile—after seventy years God started bringing them back into their land.

Based on accounts in the New Testament, Paul caused a considerable amount of suffering to Christians as a persecutor before he believed in Jesus Christ as his Savior. Then he became the recipient of even more suffering!

In 2 Corinthians 11:23-25 he describes, "I have worked much harder, been in prison more frequently, been flogged more severely, and been exposed to death again and again. Five times I received from the Jews the forty lashes minus one. Three times I was beaten with rods, once I was pelted with stones, three times I was shipwrecked; I spent a night and a day in the open sea. I have been constantly on the move. I have been in danger from rivers, in danger from bandits, in danger from my fellow Jews, in danger from Gentiles..." He goes on to list many more adversities.

More important, though, is Paul's attitude toward this suffering. He understood the eternal perspective, as is evident in Romans 8:18: "I consider that our present sufferings are not worth comparing with the glory that will be revealed in us." He knew suffering was transforming him, as we see in Romans 5:3-4: "Not only so, but we also glory in our sufferings, because we know that suffering produces perseverance; perseverance, character; and character, hope." He knew Jesus had also suffered, and now comforted him. 2 Corinthians 1:4: "For just as we share abundantly in the sufferings of Christ, so also our comfort abounds through Christ."

There are many more examples of suffering in the Bible. But no one in all of history has suffered like our Lord and Savior, Jesus Christ. His life in heaven was perfect. He lived in a wonderful loving relationship with His Father and the Holy Spirit. He is the Creator of the universe and everything in it, and He holds it all together by His word. Yet He consented to come to earth as a helpless human baby. Philippians 2:6-8: "Who being in very nature God, did not consider equality with God something to be used to His own advantage; rather, He made Himself nothing by taking the very nature of a servant, being made in human likeness. And being found in appearance as a man, He humbled Himself by becoming obedient to death—even death on a cross!" He is the only innocent person to ever inhabit a human body, and yet He suffered more than any human ever has or will.

Many people were beaten and crucified, and their physical suffering is excruciating. But Jesus is the only person to suffer unspeakably while bearing the wrath of God for us—the infinite payment for the sins of everyone ever born—on the cross. This suffering was so severe that God allowed darkness to cover it. Not only that, but to Jesus, Who had done no wrong, the incomparably painful loss of fellowship with His Father while being judged by Him caused Him to scream, "My God, My God, why have you forsaken me?" (Matthew 27:46)

No believer will ever suffer on this scale, because God remains with us in our suffering, even though he had to abandon Jesus during his.

Our God is so good! Even though there is evil, suffering, and death in the world—and it is our fault—our God is the only One powerful enough and perfectly qualified to make a way of escape for everyone, without exception, who will put their trust in Him.

How are Christians to Look at Evil and Suffering in their Lives?

Since we know that God is so wise, omnipotent, and infinite that He can use even the wrath of men to praise Him (Psalm 76:10), He is not powerless over evil. He can use evil and suffering for His own good purposes, which are eternal. We may not know what this purpose is, as Job never did. It is hard to fathom a God so infinite that He sees the past, present, and future all at one time. He knows the consequence for all time of every decision of every person. Further, He has worked all of this into His purpose—to draw many to His Son, and so to glorify His Son.

We will never know all God knows about why things are the way they are. However, He has told us what we are to think and do. Since God has not yet removed us from this evil and suffering world, what does He want our attitude to be? How can we see His mind and His purpose, and so not "waste" our suffering?

First, as believers, we may be suffering because we have turned our back on God, rejected the mandates of His word, and decided to live life on our own terms. God disciplines the people He loves, as described in Hebrews 12:7: "Endure hardship as discipline; God is treating you as his children. For what children are not disciplined by their father?" God provides a way to restore our relationship with Him, described in 1 John 1:9: "But if we confess our sins to Him, He is faithful and just to forgive us our sins and to cleanse us from all unrighteousness." We return to Him in humility, and avoid the same sins in the future, as Proverbs 15:32 tells us: "Those who disregard discipline despise themselves, but the one who heeds correction gains understanding." God will remind us to stay close in our walk with Him.

Believers who are in a growing relationship with God can be confident He knows all about their suffering and challenges. He is not standing back; He stays near. Just as Jesus wept when His friend Lazarus died, He mourns with us. He has sent the Holy Spirit as our Comforter. John 14:26: "But the Advocate [Comforter], the Holy Spirit, whom the Father will send in my name, will teach you all things and will remind you of everything I have said to you." Psalm 34:18-19: "The Lord is close to the brokenhearted and saves those who are crushed in spirit. The righteous person may have many troubles, but the Lord delivers him from them all." 2 Corinthians 12:9: "But He said to me, 'My grace is sufficient for you, for my power is made perfect in weakness.'"

God cares about our suffering. Isaiah 41:10: "So do not fear, for I am with you; do not be dismayed, for I am your God. I will strengthen you and help you; I will uphold you with my righteous right hand." Psalm 9:9-10: "The Lord is a refuge for the oppressed, a stronghold in times of trouble. Those who know your name trust in you, for you, Lord, have never forsaken those who seek you." Romans 8:35: "Who shall separate us from the love of God? Shall trouble or hardship or persecution or famine or nakedness or danger or sword?" Finally, in Romans 8:37-39, Paul explains, "No, in all these things we are more than conquerors through Him Who loved us. For I am convinced that neither death nor life, neither angels nor demons, neither the present nor the future, nor any powers, neither height nor depth, nor anything else in all creation, will be able to separate us from the love of God that is in Christ Jesus our Lord."

Most important of all, Jesus Christ suffered for us. The notion of a gracious God Who not only humbled Himself and suffered on our behalf, but stands by to comfort us in our suffering is incomprehensible to any other worldview or religious belief system. No other religion even pretends their god can eternally save man, as well as live with him in a loving relationship on earth. Hebrews 12:3: "Consider him [Jesus] who endured such opposition from sinners, so that you will not grow weary and lose heart."

To think God's way about our suffering, we need to clarify what God's will and purpose is for the believer. Jesus

183

did not arrive in His first coming as a King, but as a humble and obedient servant. That is God's desire for us. 1 John 2:6: "Whoever claims to live in him must live as Jesus did."

God's desire is to mold us into vessels He can use. He wants us to depend on Him in every circumstance, and not on ourselves. God uses suffering to build up and strengthen our trust in Him. James 1:2-4: "Consider it pure joy, my brothers and sisters, whenever you face trials of many kinds, because you know that the testing of your faith produces perseverance. Let perseverance finish its work so that you may be mature and complete, not lacking anything."

There is nothing like suffering to bring us to the end of ourselves and turn us—in complete dependence and trust—toward God. When we are powerless, He remains sufficient. He wants us to remember Who He is. He has graciously provided the Holy Spirit as our power and guide. God's desire is for us, by our own free will, to become true lovers of Him. He wants us to love and trust Him no matter what is happening to us. Then we can say, "I want Him, no matter the consequences."

Suffering will draw us to prayer as prosperity never will, as we saw with David in the Psalms. Suffering also will draw us to the comfort of His Word. As He speaks to us through the Bible, we bring our burdens to Him in prayer. These can be times of blessing like no other. Philippians 4: 6-7: "Do not be anxious about anything, but in every situation, by prayer and petition, with thanksgiving, present your requests to God. And the peace of God, which transcends all understanding, will guard your hearts and your minds in Christ Jesus." Or 1 Peter 4:7: "The end of all things is near. Therefore be alert and of sober mind so that you may pray."

Our trust and dependence on God in the midst of our suffering may serve as a witness for Christ that draws others to Him. When there is a disaster of some kind, believers who are affected may exhibit a quiet calm, trust, and perspective while there is panic all around. Isaiah 26:3: "You will keep in perfect peace those whose minds are steadfast, because they trust in you." 1 Peter 1:6-7: "In all this you greatly rejoice, though now for a little while you may have had to suffer grief in all kinds of trials. These have come so that the proven genuineness of your faith—of greater worth than gold, which perishes, even though refined by fire—may result in praise, glory, and honor when Jesus Christ is revealed."

God often uses believers as His hands and feet to minister to the helpless and hopeless. In this way, they may see God in their suffering and turn to Him for eternal salvation. We can bring comfort to the suffering because we understand and have been comforted. 2 Corinthians 1:3-4: "Praise be to the Father of our Lord Jesus Christ, the Father of compassion and God of all comfort, who comforts us in our troubles, so that we can comfort those in any trouble with the comfort we ourselves receive from God."

In times of national suffering, Christians are often known as the ones to turn to for comfort and help. God wants to show Himself to the world, and uses the hands and feet of Christians to do it. Christians often are the first on the scene of natural disasters in an attempt to relieve physical suffering by providing food or medical treatment, in the name of Jesus.

Paul tells us in Philippians 3:13, "Brothers and sisters, I do not consider myself yet to have taken hold of it. But one thing I do: Forgetting what is behind and straining toward what is ahead." We are to leave our failures in the past; do not let them steal our joy or hold us back. Instead we look forward in dependence on God. We are instructed to not worry about the future. Matthew 6:34: "Therefore do not worry about tomorrow, for tomorrow will worry about itself. Each day has enough trouble of its own." God is in control and you can trust Him.

God dwells in eternity, and He is lovingly preparing us to spend eternity with Him. We need to hang on to this eternal perspective when looking at the present evil as Paul describes in 2 Corinthians 4:16-18, "Therefore we do not lose heart. Though outwardly we are wasting away, yet inwardly we are being renewed day by day. For our light and momentary troubles are achieving for us an eternal glory that far outweighs them all. So we fix our eyes not on what is seen but on what is unseen, since what is seen is temporary, but what is unseen is eternal." The suffering of the world is just temporary for us. Philippians 3:19b-21: "Their mind is set on earthly things. But our citizenship is in heaven. And we eagerly await a Savior from there, the Lord Jesus Christ, Who, by the power that enables Him to bring everything under His control, will transform our lowly bodies so that they will be like His glorious body."

What about evil? Are we here to fight evil? God has provided the armor we need to stand against our enemies—

the world, the flesh, and the devil. This is not our fight, but God's; we stand against it, but He will conquer it. Ephesians 6:10-13: "Finally be strong in the Lord and in his mighty power. Put on the full armor of God, so that you can take your stand against the devil's schemes. For our struggle is not against flesh and blood, but against the rulers, against the authorities, against the powers of this dark world and against the spiritual forces of evil in the heavenly realms. Therefore put on the full armor of God, so that when the day of evil comes, you may be able to stand your ground, and after you have done everything, to stand."

Suffering—A Personal Application

Are you or someone in your life suffering right now? How can you use this time for the benefit of your spiritual life and even glorify God in it?

First, if someone you know and/or love is suffering suddenly, all you can do at first is just be with them. Do not try to answer their "why" questions; just be there. Let them talk if they want while you take care of the basic life functions for them. Even if they have nothing to say and you are uncomfortable, do not leave. Your inclination might be to offer a platitude or even a Bible verse, just to say something; this is not the time. You will only put up a wall and make the person feel unsafe to be real with you. Recognize and accept their emotion without judgment. Do not put a silver lining on it because there is no set timetable for grief or for "getting over" a time of suffering. Just be there until you can see it is the right time to talk and share the comfort from God that you know. This could be days or weeks or months, but trust God to let you know when.

If you yourself are suffering, this chapter is for you. Often suffering seems totally unfair. But figuring out "why" is not the real question. You must accept that you probably will not know "why" this side of heaven. Be okay without an answer, but please do not turn your back on God—He has not turned His back on you! He understands your suffering and is standing by to comfort you. He is good! Tell Him all you are feeling. Tell Him all the things you do not understand and that seem so wrong to you. Even though He already knows how you are feeling, just tell Him so it is not standing between you and Him.

Job did this, David did this, and Jeremiah did this. Many prophets poured out their hearts to God when they were suffering unjustly. God can take it! He loves you...so much in fact that He took your eternal suffering on Himself! Remember Who He is and all He has done. He wants you to trust Him because you understand Who He is, even if you do not know exactly what He is doing. This suffering will pass, if not on earth, then in eternity. Resist the temptation to fall into the sins of self-pity, unforgiveness, bitterness, or blaming others or God, as these will stall your spiritual life and spiral you downward.

When we think our suffering is too much, we are thinking of our God as too small. You already have the eternal answer.

Chapter Eight

Dare to Be a Daniel

"Dare to be a Daniel! Dare to stand alone! Dare to have a purpose firm! Dare to make it known!"

-Chorus from the hymn, "Dare to be a Daniel," Philip P. Bliss

Daniel's life, recorded in the Bible, contains timeless lessons especially pertinent for Christians in the present culture. His is a wonderful example of a life of extraordinary faith lived within a rebellious culture. In this chapter we will glean lessons from Daniel's life that will show us how to live God-honoring lives in today's world.

Background: The Babylonian Captivity

The events in the book of Daniel begin around 605 B.C. In nearly every generation since the Israelites had entered the land of Canaan, they had been worshipping idols and rebelling against God and His law. Prophets had predicted that the nation of Judah would be enslaved when they reached the point of extreme rebellion against God. In Jeremiah 25:9-12 and 29:10, the prophet predicted that the Southern Kingdom, also known as Judah, would be taken captive and enslaved in Babylon for 70 years. Isaiah predicted that Hebrew princes would be taken into captivity (Isaiah 39:7, 2 Kings 20:18). That is exactly what happened to Daniel and his three friends.

Daniel grew up in Judah and was trained in the Hebrew Bible, law, and customs. During his early years, his homeland was repeatedly invaded and plundered by the Babylonians. In 605 B.C., Daniel and three friends, as well as other teenagers of noble birth, were taken captive to the faraway land of Babylon. Ruled by King Nebuchadnezzar, Babylon was advanced in mathematics, literature, astrology, astronomy, and architecture. The Greek historian Herodotus claimed that Babylon surpassed any city in the known world. He specifically praised its walls, which he said were 56 miles long, 80 feet thick and 320 feet high. Babylon was famous for its Hanging Gardens, one of the seven wonders of the ancient world.

The Babylonians had an idolatrous worldview. Daniel was surely taught their well-known creation myth, the "Enuma Elish," about the origin of the universe and their gods. The story says their various gods were all one and came from the first god, "Nammu" (the lady of gods, also called the primeval sea), who had always existed. This sea gave birth to the universe and everything in it. In this myth, we see the rebellious idea that all is one, with everything evolving over time.

The overarching theme of the book of Daniel is that the God of Israel is sovereign over all the earth. It was this one true God Who allowed Babylon to conquer and enslave Israel. At the time, the general belief was that when a nation lost a war, it was because its god was less powerful than the god of the conquering nation. The events recounted in the book of Daniel disproved this to King Nebuchadnezzar and the rest of the world. Nebuchadnezzar could not have conquered Judah unless the true God allowed it, as God is in ultimate control of everything.

The secondary theme of the book is how to live a life of faith in a rebellious culture, and when to obey or disobey the civil government. As we will see, Daniel and his friends only disobeyed the authorities when they were ordered to do something that God had forbidden, or when the government forbade them to do what God had commanded.

Daniel Chapter One: The Character of Daniel

The young Israelite princes were captured by King Nebuchadnezzar and marched to Babylon where they were trained to be administrators to govern the Jews who would come in later waves of captivity to Babylon. For three years, Daniel and his three friends were taught the language, culture, and literature of the Babylonians in an attempt to indoctrinate them into the Babylonian idolatrous worldview.

The first test Daniel and his friends (Hananiah, Mishael, and Azariah) faced was having their Hebrew names changed to Babylonian names. Each of their Hebrew names contains a reference to the true God. Daniel means "God is my Judge." Hananiah means "God is gracious." Mishael means "who is equal to God?" Azariah means "God helps." In contrast, their new Babylonian names referred to the false gods of Babylon. Daniel's new name, Belteshazzar, means "Bel (sun god) protects his life." Hananiah became Shadrach, which means "command of Aku (the moon god)." Mishael's name was changed to Meshach, meaning "who is like Aku (the moon god)." Azariah became Abednego, or "servant of Nebo (god of wisdom and vegetation)."

The four young men did not object to the name changes, as this act was not in violation of any of God's commands. While the intent of the new names was to make them forget their belief in the one true God, they did not allow that to happen. Maintaining belief in the true God is what is important to God.

Nebuchadnezzar had confiscated valuable worship vessels from the Jewish temple and put them in the temple of the gods of Babylon. He thought the Hebrew God was nothing special, just one of many gods. Like many people today, he thought all religions are the same. Nebuchadnezzar thought he was superior to all the gods.

The food test is the second test in this chapter. Daniel refused to eat some of the food he and his friends were served. It was likely unclean according to Jewish law, and related to idolatry in some way. Daniel didn't make a big deal about it, but asked his overseer to approve a test. If after ten days on Daniel's preferred diet of water and vegetables he and his friends were healthier than the other exiles who were eating the king's diet of choice food and wine, they would be allowed to stay on the diet. After 10 days, their health was superior to those eating the king's food. Daniel's goal was to remain faithful to God, not draw attention to himself. Yet his quiet obedience was a witness noticed by men and rewarded by God. From this we learn it is not usually necessary to make a big show about resisting rules that God does not endorse.

Daniel and his three friends worked hard and earned higher grades than anyone else in their class. Daniel 1:18-20: "At the end of the time set by the king to bring them into his service, the chief official presented them to Nebuchadnezzar. The king talked with them, and he found none equal to Daniel, Hananiah, Mishael and Azariah; so they entered the king's service. In every matter of wisdom and understanding about which the king questioned them, he found them ten times better than all the magicians and enchanters in his whole kingdom."

Daniel and his friends were taught many things they knew to be false, such as evolution, astrology, magic, enchantments, and idolatry. They did not refuse to learn these things—they memorized and passed the tests, but it did not affect their fundamental beliefs and faith.

Today's students can apply this same practice as they learn all they are taught, even when they know some of it is wrong or non-Biblical. Our purpose in life remains the same in any circumstance—to serve and glorify the Lord.

Daniel Chapter Two: Nebuchadnezzar's Dream

One night Nebuchadnezzar had a disturbing dream and he demanded his wise men tell him what the dream was, as well as what it meant. They told him this was an impossible request as only the gods knew what he had dreamed. Nebuchadnezzar ordered the execution of all the wise men. Daniel asked the king to wait and he would tell the king what his dream was and interpret it. That night, before he met with the king, Daniel joined with his friends in a prayer meeting. Praying and group prayers are indispensable in times of testing. God dramatically answered their prayer by revealing the dream and its interpretation to Daniel.

Nebuchadnezzar had dreamed about a huge statue made of different parts, each with a prophetic meaning.

From verses 32-35: "The head was made of pure gold [meaning the Babylonian empire], its chest and arms of silver [Medo-Persian empire], its belly and thighs of bronze [Greek empire], its legs of iron [Roman empire], and its feet partly of iron and partly of baked clay [future empire of the Anti-Christ]." Then a rock [Jesus Christ] cut "not by human hands" hit the foot of the statue, and the whole image broke up and "became like chaff on a threshing floor." The rock "became a huge mountain and filled the whole earth."

This dream prophetically describes how Jesus will destroy all the earthly kingdoms at the future battle of Armageddon and set up his 1,000-year reign over the entire earth.

Nebuchadnezzar fell down on his face at the feet of Daniel, saying, "Surely your God is the God of gods and the Lord of kings and a revealer of mysteries, for you were able to reveal this mystery." The king promoted Daniel over the province of Babylon, put him in charge of all the wise men, and lavished many gifts on him. At Daniel's request, the king appointed Shadrach, Meshach, and Abednego administrators over the province of Babylon, while Daniel remained in the royal court. Daniel remembered his friends and helped them to get better jobs. There is nothing wrong with career networking among fellow Christians!

Daniel's prayer of thanksgiving is found in verses 20-23: "Blessed be the name of God forever and ever, for wisdom and might are His. He changes the times and the seasons; He removes kings and raises up kings; He gives wisdom to the wise, and knowledge to those who have understanding. He reveals deep and secret things; He knows what is in the darkness, and light dwells with Him. I thank You and praise You, O God of my fathers; You have given me wisdom and might, and have now made known to me what we asked of You, For You have made known to us the king's demand."

Daniel provides a wonderful example of prayer before testing and then praise after God answers! This prayer shows Daniel understood God's character and that God is sovereign over all.

Daniel Chapter Three: The Fiery Furnace

Nebuchadnezzar decided to build a huge statue, similar to the one in his dream, but made completely of gold. I believe this demonstrated his hope that his empire would not be replaced, but would continue forever. He decreed that everyone in the area must bow down to the statue every time his band played music.

God's law, as laid out in Exodus 20:4 and Leviticus 26:1, specifically forbids bowing down to idols. Daniel's three friends followed God's law and refused to bow down. They chose to obey the higher law of God rather than the arbitrary laws of a man. Some people who were probably jealous of the three friends reported to the king that they were not bowing down.

As a result, the king called them, as we read in verses 13-15: "Furious with rage, Nebuchadnezzar summoned Shadrach, Meshach and Abednego. So these men were brought before the king, and Nebuchadnezzar said to them, 'Is it true, Shadrach, Meshach and Abednego, that you do not serve my gods or worship the image of gold I have set up? Now when you hear the sound of the horn, flute, zither, lyre, harp, pipe and all kinds of music, if you are ready to fall down and worship the image I made, very good. But if you do not worship it, you will be thrown immediately into a blazing furnace. Then what god will be able to rescue you from my hand?'" Nebuchadnezzar clearly believed his hand was more powerful than any god and he angrily gave them one more chance to follow his orders.

The three young men had studied the Scriptures and the promise given in Isaiah 43:2: "I will be with you...When you walk through the fire, you will not be burned; the flames will not set you ablaze." We hear their response in verses 16-18: "Shadrach, Meshach and Abednego replied to him, 'King Nebuchadnezzar, we do not need to defend ourselves before you in this matter. If we are thrown into the blazing furnace, the God we serve is able to deliver us from it, and he will deliver us from Your Majesty's hand. But even if he does not, we want you to know, Your Majesty, that we will not serve your gods or worship the image of gold you have set up.'"

They knew their God was able to save them and they were fully trusting God regardless of what God chose to do. The king had the furnace heated to seven times the normal temperature. It was so hot that the soldiers who threw them in died. Next, in verses 24-27: "Then King Nebuchadnezzar leaped to his feet in amazement and asked his advisers, 'Weren't there three men that we tied up and threw into the fire?' They replied, 'Certainly, Your Majesty.' He said, 'Look! I see four men walking around in the fire, unbound and unharmed, and the fourth looks like a son of the gods.'

Nebuchadnezzar then approached the opening of the blazing furnace and shouted, 'Shadrach, Meshach and Abednego, servants of the Most High God, come out! Come here!' So Shadrach, Meshach and Abednego came out of the fire, and the satraps, prefects, governors and royal advisers crowded around them. They saw that the fire had not harmed their bodies, nor was a hair of their heads singed; their robes were not scorched, and there was no smell of fire on them."

God was with them. I believe Jesus Christ was the fourth person in the furnace. They were not burned or set ablaze, as the promise in Isaiah stated. This was a major miracle performed before the king and a large crowd. The king's reaction is recorded in verse 28: "Then Nebuchadnezzar said, 'Praise be to the God of Shadrach, Meshach and Abednego, who has sent his angel and rescued his servants! They trusted in him and defied the king's command and were willing to give up their lives rather than serve or worship any god except their own God.'" Nebuchadnezzar acknowledged that the God of Israel was great, but he still thought of himself as greater.

Daniel's friends trusted God with their very lives. God can be trusted. Proverbs 3:5-6: "Trust in the Lord with all your heart and lean not on your own understanding; in all your ways submit to Him, and He will make your paths straight."

Daniel Chapter Four: Nebuchadnezzar's Insanity

In Daniel 4 we see Nebuchadnezzar praising himself for his great and universal rule over the earth. But then he had a disturbing dream of a great towering tree that was cut down by a messenger, a holy one. His wise men were not able to interpret the dream, so Daniel was called and he once again used his God-given ability to interpret it.

Verses 19-25: "Daniel answered, 'My lord, if only the dream applied to your enemies and its meaning to your adversaries! The tree you saw, which grew large and strong, with its top touching the sky, visible to the whole earth, with beautiful leaves and abundant fruit, providing food for all, giving shelter to the wild animals, and having nesting places in its branches for the birds—Your Majesty, you are that tree! You have become great and strong; your greatness has grown until it reaches the sky, and your dominion extends to distant parts of the earth. Your Majesty saw a holy one, a messenger, coming down from heaven and saying, 'Cut down the tree and destroy it, but leave the stump, bound with iron and bronze, in the grass of the field, while its roots remain in the ground. Let him be drenched with the dew of heaven; let him live with the wild animals, until seven times pass by for him.' This is the interpretation, Your Majesty, and this is the decree the Most High has issued against my lord the king: You will be driven away from people and will live with the wild animals; you will eat grass like the ox and be drenched with the dew of heaven. Seven times will pass by for you until you acknowledge that the Most High is sovereign over all kingdoms on earth and gives them to anyone he wishes."

This prophetic dream was fulfilled a year later when Nebuchadnezzar became temporarily insane (lycanthropy) and acted like an animal for seven years.

Nebuchadnezzar finally came to his senses and realized the supremacy of the God of Israel, as we see in verses 34-37: "At the end of that time, I, Nebuchadnezzar, raised my eyes toward heaven, and my sanity was restored. Then I praised the Most High; I honored and glorified him who lives forever. His dominion is an eternal dominion; his kingdom endures from generation to generation. All the peoples of the earth are regarded as nothing. He does as he pleases with the powers of heaven and the peoples of the earth. No one can hold back his hand or say to him: 'What have you done?'....Now I, Nebuchadnezzar, praise and exalt and glorify the King of heaven, because everything he does is right and all his ways are just. And those who walk in pride he is able to humble."

Daniel Chapter Five: Belshazzar's Feast

The events in Chapter 5 occur at a later time, when Daniel was probably around eighty years old. He was serving under King Belshazzar, the son or possibly the grandson of King Nebuchadnezzar. Belshazzar had not learned the lesson Nebuchadnezzar had learned—that the God of Israel was sovereign over all. Belshazzar thought his kingdom was invincible; he had a huge wall around the city. At this time Darius and the Persians were preparing to attack, but Belshazzar held a big party. He called for the gold and silver goblets that had been taken from the temple in Jerusalem so that the king, his nobles, his wives, and his concubines might drink from them. They were desecrating the holy vessels and mocking the God of Israel.

Suddenly a hand appeared and wrote a message on the wall. Belshazzar's wise men were unable to interpret the message for the king.

The queen mother suggested that Daniel be called to tell them what it meant. Daniel was offered a great reward to do so, which he declined, but he told the king the meaning in verse 26: "God has numbered the days of your reign and brought it to an end. You have been weighed on the scales and found wanting. Your kingdom is divided and given to the Medes and Persians." That night the city was overrun and King Belshazzar was killed. The message to the world is that it isn't a good idea to mock the God of Israel. Even though God allowed Babylon to conquer Judah, God eventually judged Babylon as well. God alone determines the rise and fall of nations, and all rulers serve His purpose.

Daniel Chapter Six: Daniel in the Den of Lions

The conquering Medo-Persian king, Darius, recognized Daniel's ability and integrity, and assigned him one of the top three government jobs. He performed his duties faithfully and expertly and became very successful, so much so that the other two leaders became jealous. They tried without success to find fault with Daniel. Since he was above reproach, they set a trap.

They had seen Daniel pray to his God three times a day from his window, while facing Jerusalem. They advised King Darius to decree that for thirty days no one was to pray to any god or man besides the king. Anyone who did would be thrown into the lions' den. The king, in his pride, signed the decree into law. Immediately the conspirators spied on

Daniel, observed him praying, and reported back to the king in verse 13, "Daniel, who is one of the exiles from Judah, pays no attention to you, Your Majesty, or to the decree you put in writing. He still prays to his God three times a day." The king was not happy to hear this this because he liked Daniel, but under the law there was nothing that he could do.

Verse 16: "So the king gave the order, and they brought Daniel and threw him into the lions' den. The king said to Daniel, 'May your God, whom you serve continually, rescue you!'" Daniel spent the night peacefully in the lion's den. After a sleepless night, the king hurried to the den in the morning and anxiously called out (verse 20): "Daniel, servant of the living God, has your God, whom you serve continually, been able to rescue you from the lions?" Daniel responded that God had sent an angel to keep the mouths of the lions shut. The king was ecstatic! He commanded that the men who had accused Daniel be thrown into the lions' den, and before their bodies reached the floor they were caught and killed.

God's sovereignty over all of creation was demonstrated—God prevented the lions from killing Daniel. Darius learned that the God of Israel is sovereign, and he proclaims in verses 26-27, "'I issue a decree that in every part of my kingdom people must fear and reverence the God of Daniel. For he is the living God and he endures forever; his kingdom will not be destroyed, his dominion will never end. He rescues and he saves; he performs signs and wonders in the heavens and on the earth. He has rescued Daniel from the power of the lions.'"

The story of Daniel teaches us that even when living and working in a rebellious society, we are God's ambassadors. We may be held to a higher standard but we are to live lives of integrity and honor, doing our jobs as unto the Lord, even when those around us are doing wrong or even maligning us. Our accountability is to God, as Paul describes in 1 Corinthians 10:31, "So, whether you eat or drink, or whatever you do, do all to the glory of God." Whether we are rewarded or unjustly punished in this world is in God's hands alone.

Daniel Chapters 7-12: Daniel's Apocalyptic Visions and Israel's Future in Prophecy

These chapters are foundational to understanding Biblical prophecy related to the future of Israel and the end times of our age. Daniel received several prophetic visions directly from God. These chapters are written in apocalyptic style, characterized by the extensive use of symbols that complement each other to convey a message.

For example, notice Daniel's vision described in Chapter 8. He saw a ram with two horns, one larger than the other and it charged to the west, north, and south, and no animal could stand against it. Then a goat with a single horn flew into the picture, charged the ram and destroyed it. The goat was very great but at the height of its power the horn was broken off and four prominent horns grew.

This prophecy, in fact, has been fulfilled. We now know that the ram represented the Medo-Persian Empire and the lands they conquered. The goat represents Alexander the Great and his rapid conquest of the known world followed by his early death, represented by the broken horn. The four horns that replaced it are the four generals who took his place in his empire after his death.

While this and other detailed prophecies found in these last six chapters have already been fulfilled, others are still in the future. These prophecies assured the Hebrew people that their exile in Babylon would end. God had not forgotten the promise He made to Jeremiah that the people would return to their land after 70 years of captivity.

Notice also Daniel's prayer for Israel in Chapter 9:4-19. He confesses the disobedience of Israel which led to their captivity and appeals to God's perfect character and mercy. Daniel thought the Messiah would be coming after the 70 years of captivity. In response, God gave Daniel the "seventy weeks" promise—the precise timeline of when the Messiah would come (69 times 7, or 483 years after the order from a future king to restore and rebuild the city of Jerusalem), and then be cut off (crucified).

The seventieth week, known in Revelation as the great tribulation, would be delayed until just before Jesus comes again. A future ruler, the Anti-Christ, will make a seven-year covenant with Israel at the beginning of the tribulation period but he will break the agreement after three and a half years. The following three and a half years will be filled with great judgments and trouble until the end of the tribulation when Jesus Christ, the Messiah, returns to conquer and rule. The message is a reminder to the Jewish people and to all people that God is still in charge; His plan will be carried out. He never forgets His promises and their fulfillment depends on His character, which is perfect.

The angel Gabriel comes to strengthen Daniel and explain the visions to him. We gain insight into the invisible conflict—the angelic warfare raging in heaven as well as on earth. The angel was delayed for 21 days by the King of Persia (likely Satan or an evil angel), but was able to reach Daniel with the help of the archangel Michael. God is in control and will prevail. No matter how bad things get in the present or the future, our God will ultimately be victorious. We are on the winning team and our role is to do as He assigns us as His witnesses and ambassadors on this earth.

When Daniel saw how awesome God is, he could do nothing but fall on his face, as his strength left him. The more we understand and know our God, the more we will be able to do nothing else but worship Him.

Personal Application

The book of Daniel is a wonderful comfort for us. We see that God is sovereign over all; He is in control. Your life will not be free of problems—life on this fallen planet never is. You will surely face personal problems and challenges of many kinds. There may be manmade or natural catastrophes affecting you in your lifetime as well. The one sure thing is that you can trust God. Understand that the testing of your faith, if you continue to rely on and obey God, will result in an even more confident trust in God. The peace you can have in difficult times will be a light that shines out to the world.

Remembering Daniel's example, we too can live an effective spiritual life in a rebellious culture. Daniel could have dwelt on how unfair his captivity was, but he focused on trusting and obeying God. God gives us the ability through His Holy Spirit to live before Him honorably as we use His power and trust His word, the Bible. Even in a hostile environment full of pressure to conform, Daniel and his three friends were able to live a life of faith and maintain a close walk with their Lord. While in captivity, the four did not keep their faith private but maintained a high-profile public witness within an idolatrous society. God put them in positions of power and influence even as the surrounding world grew antagonistic toward them.

My hope and prayer is that you will impact the world around you—that you will be a "Daniel" for your generation. "Dare to be a Daniel! Dare to stand alone! Dare to have a purpose firm! Dare to make it known!"

Our culture is becoming more and more rebellious towards God—holding to political correctness over Biblical values, exerting pressure to keep faith private, and stifling and distorting our witness to the lost and dying world. You are called to be strong and courageous and let your light shine. You may have failures, but keep your focus on God and His provision, His Word, and His plan for you and all of history. May you be encouraged as you study the faithful heroes like Daniel who have led the way!

Chapter Nine

A Life Plan with Purpose

"If Christianity should happen to be true—that is to say, if its God is the real God of the universe—then defending it may mean talking about anything and everything. Things can be irrelevant to the proposition that Christianity is false, but nothing can be irrelevant to the proposition that Christianity is true."

- G.K. Chesterton

"We are destroying speculations and every lofty thing raised up against the knowledge of God, and we are taking every thought captive to the obedience of Christ."

-2 Corinthians 10:5

The Importance of Being a Witness for Christ

This chapter will help you prepare to share your Christian faith in college, the workplace, and wherever else you go in life. Having placed your faith in Jesus Christ as your Savior, the expectation is that for the rest of your life on earth you will be continually transformed by the renewing of your mind with God's truth, learning to trust Him, obey Him, and serve Him.

It is also possible to ignore God and your faith, and live a life that can't be distinguished from the rest of the world. This is shortsighted because in eternity your status in the new heaven and earth will be determined by how well you served your Savior during your time on the earth.

This chapter will assume your intention is to obey the parting command of our Lord Jesus Christ in Matthew 28:19-20 when He said, "Therefore, go and make disciples of all nations, baptizing them in the name of the Father and of the Son and of the Holy Spirit, and teaching them to obey everything I have commanded you. And surely I am with you always, even to the end of the age." You have the truth, the very word of God, the eternal hope every heart is searching for, and the power of His Spirit in you. This chapter will present ideas of how to share that truth effectively.

Keeping the Right Attitude

Your overarching goal is always to glorify God in all that you do. The power is God's, not yours. It is essential to seek God in prayer for the lost souls you know, and ask Him to put others in your path. As you make yourself available in obedience, the Holy Spirit will do the work through you.

Our mission is not to defeat anyone, but to gently point out their errors in thinking. 1 Peter 3:15: "But in your hearts revere Christ as Lord. Always be prepared to give an answer to everyone who asks you to give the reason for the hope that you have. But do this with gentleness and respect."

Jesus describes our mission in Matthew 10:16: "Behold, I send you out as sheep in the midst of wolves; so be shrewd as serpents and innocent as doves." We are instructed to be wise but also gentle. Wisdom is essential, as we see in Colossians 4:5-6: "Conduct yourselves with wisdom toward outsiders, making the most of the opportunity. Let your speech always be with grace, as though seasoned with salt, so that you will know how you should respond to each person."

A Good Listener and Questioner

My first suggestion is to cultivate the art of being a good listener. Listening with an open mind will expand your own knowledge, give insight into the other person's motivations, and bring a deeper understanding of his or her needs and burdens. James 1:19 tells us, "My dear brothers and sisters, take note of this: Everyone should be quick to listen, slow to speak and slow to become angry."

Along with listening, learn to ask good questions. When you are asked a question, the best response may be to ask a clarifying question. Words carry meanings and assumptions that may be different for different people. Defining the terms you both are using will often bring common ground from which to start the discussion. The real differences in beliefs will be highlighted when each of you understand the words and assumptions of the other.

God used this questioning method when He answered Job's questions with 64 questions of His own starting in Job 38:4-5. "Where were you when I laid the foundation of the earth? Tell me, if you have understanding. Who determined its measurements—surely you know! Or who stretched the line upon it?"

Jesus used the same method when He was a twelve-year old boy in the temple. Luke 2:46-47: "After three days

209

they found him in the temple courts, sitting among the teachers, *listening to them and asking them questions.* Everyone who heard him was amazed at his understanding and his answers."

As recorded in the gospels, Jesus answered questions with questions approximately 90% of the time. For example, when he was asked by the rich young ruler, "Good master what must I do to be saved?" Jesus responded by asking, "Why do you call me good, there is none good but God?" On another occasion, Jesus was asked, "Is it right to pay taxes to Caesar or not?" Jesus' response was to ask, "Whose portrait is on the coin?" When Pilate asked Jesus, "Are you king of the Jews?" Jesus replied with a question of his own: "Is that your idea or did others talk to you about me?"

Various ministries suggest a three step questioning method that I have found to be quite effective. When someone asks a question or makes what you believe to be an incorrect statement, ask a clarifying question, such as, "Tell me what you mean by that?" Ask the person for more details or to define a specific term in their question or statement. This will ensure you are both talking about the same thing. When asked in a non-threatening way, most people will take this as a show of interest in their views. It is important to listen carefully so you can understand and ask good questions. Don't assume you know what people mean but reflect their views back to them to make *sure* you understand.

The second step is to ask for further information, such as, "How did you come to that conclusion?" or "How do you know that to be true?" In this way you will see how the person arrived at the conclusion; this also tells you what evidence he or she may have for their claims. Your aim here is to understand the person's thought process.

The third step is to suggest an alternative belief by asking, "Have you ever considered...?" Fill in the rest of the sentence with reasonable facts or a truth claim that is an alternative to the beliefs of that person.

How these steps work

Here is a possible scenario. What if someone challenges you with, "The Bible has changed so many times over the years." Your first response could be to ask, "What do you mean it has been changed?" Then proceed to the next step. "How do you know that it changed without an earlier reference?" Finally, you could ask, "Have you considered the accuracy of manuscripts found from various locations and periods, some very close to the time the originals were written?"

Suppose someone states that "No one can know the truth about religion." You might ask, "What do you mean by truth?" Or, "What is your definition of religion?" Follow up with, "How did you come to know this?" Finally, ask, "Have you considered or compared the truth claims and evidences for the various religions?"

No doubt at some point in your life you will hear a statement such as, "Evolution is a proven fact." I would respond, "What do you mean by evolution?" followed by, "How did the evolution process start? Do you believe that molecules turned into living cells and then humans by random chance?" Finally, zero in on the issues by asking,

"Have you considered the possibility that there may have been a supernatural first cause?"

These are questions designed to get people to think, not points to argue. Many people believe what they have been told without really evaluating the evidence or likelihood that it is true. Others, however, have a moral reason to reject the truth—they will hold on to even irrational beliefs because they do not want to be held accountable to the Creator God.

Questions about Morality

Moral issues are frequently used against Christians. Beyond the "what, and how, and have you considered" questions, a good model of how to best answer this type of question comes from Christian apologist Greg Koukl, who recommends, "If you're placed in a situation where you suspect your convictions will be labeled intolerant, bigoted, narrow-minded, and judgmental, turn the tables. When someone asks for your personal views about a moral issue—homosexuality, for example, preface your remarks with a question. You say: 'You know, this is actually a very personal question you're asking, and I'd be glad to answer. But before I do, I want to know if you consider yourself a tolerant person or an intolerant person. Is it safe to give my opinion, or are you going to judge me for my point of view? Do you respect diverse ideas, or do you condemn others for convictions that differ from yours?' Let them answer. If they say they're tolerant (which they probably will), then when you give your point of view it's going to be very difficult for them to call you intolerant or judgmental without looking guilty, too. This response capitalizes on the fact that there's no morally neutral ground. Everybody has a point of view they think is right and everybody judges at some point or another. The Christian gets pigeon-holed as the judgmental one, but everyone else is judging, too. It's an inescapable consequence of believing in any kind of morality."

Personal Evangelism

As Christians, our mission is to cooperate with the Holy Spirit to bring lost sinners to faith in Christ and then to disciple them. Jesus tells us of the eternal and invisible significance of personal evangelism in Luke 15:10: "In the same way, I tell you, there is rejoicing in the presence of the angels of God over one sinner who repents." It is God's desire that all should come to a saving knowledge of His Son.

Cultural differences and changes bring new challenges to evangelism. Earlier in our country's history, Bible reading and prayer were daily occurrences in public schools. Most people were conscious of God. Now the dominant culture has moved away from the Biblical worldview. Fewer people believe in God or even see a need for God in their lives. Everyone does what is right in their own eyes and they like it! This is why our approach to evangelism must adapt and it becomes necessary to start with the reality of the Creator God of the Bible.

Peter and Paul sought to reach different cultural groups in the book of Acts. In Acts 2, Peter preached the gospel to Jews, and 3,000 became believers in Jesus Christ. In contrast, when Paul reasoned with the Greeks on Mars Hill in Athens in Acts 17, perhaps 5 or 6 became believers.

The two groups had different worldviews and different hurdles to overcome. The Jews already believed in God and knew the Hebrew Scripture. Peter primarily needed to teach the truth about Jesus and the imperative to trust in Him. On the other hand, the Greeks believed in many gods but not the God of the Bible. Paul started where the Greeks were at culturally. He noticed their unknown god and explained to them that his God was the Creator God. Eventually Paul was able to explain how God's Son came to the earth, died for them on the cross and was resurrected from the grave. Paul had to go back to creation and explain God's redemptive plan for humanity. As we see in 1 Corinthians 1:23: "But we preach Christ crucified: a stumbling block to Jews and foolishness to Gentiles."

Our country today has moved from a Jewish-type culture (Biblical worldview) to a Greek culture (non-Biblical worldview). This means we need to go back further in God's truth to find common ground to begin reasoning—to the creation of the universe in most cases. Paul reasoned with the Athenians and he gave logical evidence in a persuasive manner without arguing or insulting them.

Personal evangelism in today's culture usually starts with our living a righteous life. As Jesus says in Matthew 5:16, "Let your light shine before others, that they may see your good deeds and glorify your Father in heaven." By living in a virtuous way, holding yourself to a high moral standard, and exhibiting the fruits of the Spirit in your everyday life at school, home, or work, you can be a witness to the love of Christ for the world. Of course none of us are perfect, but part of our witness is also how we acknowledge, apologize for, and make right our failures. Your life should look different so that people will wonder why.

Besides your life witness, be ready to have meaningful conversations with unbelievers anywhere or anytime you cross paths. Do you know what you would say if you are sitting next to a stranger in an airplane, at a neighborhood function, or during a social gathering? Would you know how to start a conversation that leads to the gospel? Some like to jump right in and give the gospel, but without love and personal understanding this witness can come across as offensive. 1 Corinthians 13:1: "If I speak with the tongues of men and of angels, but do not have love, I have become a noisy gong or a clanging cymbal."

A good way to begin these conversations is asking questions in a friendly way. Ask where they are from and what is going on in their lives. Take as much time as you can to get to know the person. Find out where God is working in his or her life, where they have needs, and join Him there.

Eventually, as the Holy Spirit leads, you may turn the conversation to spiritual things. You may ask: What do they think the meaning of life is? Do they have any religious beliefs? Do they believe in God? If they do not believe in God, you might ask how they think the universe came into being or how did life begin? Be prepared to respond to doubts and suggest reasonable answers. This is where apologetics becomes a part of evangelism. This is why we spent so much time in the previous chapters teaching the evidence for God and why we believe the Bible is His Word.

It is very important not to jump ahead, but to stay on common or neutral ground. They are not ready to hear the plan of salvation if they do not believe in a Creator God or that the Bible is His inspired Word. If they do believe in God and His Word, ask if anyone has ever shown them from the Bible how they can know for sure they are going to heaven. Let them read aloud some salvation verses. It is good to carry a Bible and be ready for this. You may use verses like John 3:16, 36: "For God so loved the world that he gave his one and only Son that whoever believes in him shall not perish but have eternal life....Whoever believes in the Son has eternal life, but whoever rejects the Son will not see life, for God's wrath remains on him."

"Bad news, good news" is another approach. Suggest they read these verses aloud. Romans 3:23: "For all have sinned and fall short of the glory of God." Romans 6:23: "For the wages of sin is death, but the gift of God is eternal life in Christ Jesus our Lord." Romans 5:8: "But God demonstrates his own love for us in this: While we were still sinners, Christ died for us." Ephesians 2:8-9: "For it is by grace you have been saved, through faith—and this not from yourselves, it is the gift of God, not by works, so that no one can boast."

Do they understand those verses? The way of salvation is faith alone in Christ alone as the Son of God, their personal Savior who paid the price for their sins on the cross and rose from the grave. Next I would ask, "Is there anything that is keeping you from trusting in Christ right now?" If they indicate they are not ready, there may be questions you need to address. If they indicate they are ready to trust in Christ, take some time to go over what they believe, having them articulate the gospel to you. Ask if they would like to pray out loud to God expressing their faith. Make sure they know it is not the prayer that saves them but their faith alone in Christ alone. There will be much rejoicing in heaven and on earth when this happens! Take time and invite them to church and talk about the Bible, God's instructions for their lives.

So why not just start off with the simple gospel message? I tried that with literally hundreds of people with very little effect. I started to have doubts, and in prayer asked God what I could do to change the way I witnessed. The next Sunday I found a cassette message about "Starting and Ending a Conversation about God" from Larry Moyer and his ministry, Evantell.org, on an information table at church. This lesson, as I have described it above, greatly influenced me and I have used it since. I'm blessed to have been used by God to lead many individuals to Christ. Be ready, pray for courage and opportunity, and the Lord will send people your way. For more information, check out www.evantell.org.

Special Advice for College Students Engaging Professors

Public universities have a rich heritage of promoting free speech. They were once a "marketplace of ideas." But today, at many universities, one group of students is marginalized, silenced, and even mocked—namely, Christians, especially Christians that are creationists.

217

Retired law professor and author, Dr. Phillip E. Johnson explains: "Creationists are disqualified from making a positive case, because science by definition is based upon naturalism. The rules of science also disqualify any purely negative argumentation designed to dilute the persuasiveness of the theory of evolution. Creationism is thus out of court—and out of the classroom—before any consideration of evidence. Put yourself in the place of a creationist who has been silenced by that logic, and you may feel like a criminal defendant who has just been told that the law does not recognize so absurd a concept as 'innocence.'"

Your interactions in college will not necessarily be fair. As Jesus tells us in John 16:33, "In this world you will have trouble. But take heart! I have overcome the world." Remember that absolute truth is on your side, as well as the Author of all truth!

Following the example of Daniel and his friends, your goal should be to do the best you can, earning the best grades you are able to achieve. Become proficient in your area of study and prepare yourself to be a positive influence wherever God uses you in the future. Proverbs 22:29: "Do you see someone skilled in their work? They will serve before kings; they will not serve before officials of low rank."

In your college career it is important to make connections with other Christians in various Christian organizations and a local church. Daniel and his friends encouraged each other, praying together, studying together, and building each other up in the faith.

It is also important to become a good questioner in class; this will help you think through an idea and understand it rather than just accept information that may or may not be true.

An interviewer once asked Isidor I. Rabi, a Nobel Prize winner, how he became a scientist. Rabi replied that every day after school his mother would ask, "Did you ask a good question today?" "Asking good questions," Rabi said, "made me become a scientist." There is nothing wrong with asking questions, depending on the size of the class. You are there to learn all you can, so ask good questions in class in order to learn, not to trigger an argument or confrontation, even if much of what you are learning is incorrect thinking. Observing how false thinking makes incorrect assumptions and justifies itself can be valuable knowledge. The battle for the truth of the Bible should not be in the classroom but in individual evangelism outside the classroom.

You are likely to encounter professors with an anti-God worldview and it is important to be prepared. Some professors have announced at the start of classes, "If you believe in God, you will fail this class." You are very likely to be ostracized and marginalized in this class, so as the Holy Spirit leads, you might register for a different professor.

A sociology professor once made this statement in the syllabus for his class: "Except to one whose reason is blinded by unquestioning adherence to fundamentalist doctrines of creation, the evidence of the fossil record, with that of anatomy, embryology, biochemistry and genetics, compels a single conclusion: evolution is a fact." Professors like this are not going to be open to any evidence for God. They truly believe they are going to make the world a better place by inculcating their worldview in their students.

In "A Religion for a New Age," published in The Humanist magazine, John J. Dunphy, a devout humanist, describes this agenda very clearly: "I am convinced that the battle for humankind's future must be waged and won in the public school classroom by teachers who correctly perceive their role as the proselytizers of a new faith: a religion of humanity that recognizes and respects the spark of what theologians call divinity in every human being. These teachers must embody the same selfless dedication as the most rabid fundamentalist preachers, for they will be ministers of another sort, utilizing a classroom instead of a pulpit to convey humanist values in whatever subject they teach, regardless of the educational level—preschool day care or large state university. The classroom must and will become an arena of conflict between the old and the new— the rotting corpse of Christianity, together with all its adjacent evils and misery, and the new faith of humanism..."

Richard Dawkins, Professor at Oxford, also believes Christianity is the problem, as he states in his book The God Delusion: "Faith is one of the world's great evils, comparable to the smallpox virus but harder to eradicate. Religion is capable of driving people to such dangerous folly that faith seems to me to qualify as a kind of mental illness."

Not all professors will be as extreme as these two, but you may well meet some who clearly think Christianity is what is wrong with the world. Their classroom is not where the battle should be fought. I suggest you learn all you can from these professors and just ask good questions.

If you are questioned by a professor about your faith, tell him or her that you are there to learn and not to teach. If you are treated badly or persecuted because of your faith, you have on your side the Civil Rights Act of 1964 that outlaws discrimination based on religion (page 29, Section 703). If you are being discriminated against, start recording the encounters on your smart phone to document your case, then contact a Christian legal assistance organization.

Perhaps you've seen the movie "God is Not Dead." In it, the professor asks everyone to write on the topic, "God is dead." One Christian student refused. The professor invited him to explain his beliefs to the class for 15 minutes in the next couple of classes. The student agreed and he gave arguments for the existence of God and creation, and did a very fine job. The professor might have expected the student to give a message about Christianity rather than zeroing in on the science related to creation and the universe—an apologetics message. I doubt you will ever be put in this position, but it is a great example of going back further to find neutral, objective common ground and a place of initial agreement.

In my own experience in graduate school at Sam Houston State University, our class was instructed to read the novel Ishmael by Daniel Quinn. In the story a writer answers an ad seeking a writer and meets a gorilla named Ishmael. Ishmael is able to communicate with the author telepathically and he tells the writer he wants him to write a book that he will dictate. The writer agrees. The majority of the book is a record of the telepathic dialogue between Ishmael and the writer.

The book presents Darwinian evolution as the truth of origins. Ishmael attributes all global problems throughout history to domination of the "wrong" worldview (without naming it, he is referring to the Biblical worldview). He claims that if everyone shared his belief system, these problems would never have happened.

Ishmael verifies his assertions with examples, such as the mysterious disappearance of the lost Hopi Indian tribe, which he asserted his worldview would have prevented. He lists other cultures that have disappeared without explanation. All of his examples are non-falsifiable (unprovable either way) as we don't know what really happened with these cultures. Of course, he could have used real life examples that were verifiable, but chose not to as the facts would show his worldview doesn't work. Ishmael wants to warn the world to adopt his worldview to address the problems of the world. The writer never questions the teachings of the gorilla, but dutifully records them in the book he was commissioned to write.

After reading the book, we were each given 10 minutes to give an oral review of the book to the class. The professor specifically said we were not to use the Bible in refuting the ideas given in the book. Obviously he recognized the worldview of the book was counter to what the Bible had to say. When it was my turn to address the class, I illustrated the book's absurdity with an absurdity of my own, a technique known as reduction to absurdity, or argument to absurdity, or "answer a fool according to his own folly," as described in Proverbs 26:4-5. This takes the other person's idea to its logical conclusion, showing it is absurd.

I told the class I wanted to find a nice relaxing spot to read and enjoy the book, so I travelled to the nearby Gulf coast and walked out to the end of a pier. While I was reading the book, I told them, a dolphin came by and interrupted. He started to communicate with me telepathically! I told the dolphin I was reading the book Ishmael. The dolphin told me he had read it. He asked me what I thought of it and I told him it seemed pretty convincing. He asked me what proof did the author give and I told him how he used examples of extinct civilizations which were destroyed by a bad worldview. The dolphin confided in me that those civilizations had all been visited by a gorilla like Ishmael and subsequently adopted his cultural worldview, which, in fact, led to their destruction!

In my story the dolphin went on to describe the proper worldview that would have prevented that destruction, and what we needed to implement in our society today. I asked the dolphin why I should believe him, rather than Ishmael, and he said because dolphins are smarter than gorillas. After finishing my story everybody had a pretty good laugh. I think the Holy Spirit had a hand in coming up with the story. For the rest of my ten minutes I went on to say why I didn't think Ishmael's ideas were all that great and brought out real historical events that were the result of his worldview. It was a fun exercise and some of the students liked it but the professor did not. I think it caused my grade to drop a little but I don't regret doing it!

You never know what doors God will open for you. If you are prepared, don't be surprised when God uses you! I found an interesting story on YouTube, titled: "Atheist Dr. Richard Lumsden Biology Professor Converts to Christianity." Dr. Lumsden was a professor of parasitology and cell biology at Tulane University in Louisiana. A student approached him after he mocked Christianity during a class. The student wasn't defensive or argumentative, but instead asked some very good questions along the lines of: You taught that mutations are genetic disasters—how were they able to generate improved structures through natural selection? Isn't the random assembly of genes physically and chemically and mathematically impossible? Where in the fossil record is the evidence for progressive evolution, the transitional forms between the major groups?

They had a long conversation and the professor came to the conclusion that evolution was not based on good science. He literally said, "Oh My God!" realizing this was the only alternative explanation. He came to the conclusion of Romans 1:22: "Professing themselves to be wise, they became fools." Dr. Lumsden eventually became a creationist, then a believer in Jesus Christ. He went on to debate atheists, defending the Biblical worldview, working for I.C.R. for several years. He died in 1997.

Don't assume God can't use you in special ways because you don't know it all. Paul says in 1 Corinthians 1:26-29, "Brothers, think of what you were when you were called. Not many of you were wise by human standards; not many were influential; not many were of noble birth. But

God chose the foolish things of the world to shame the wise; God chose the weak things of the world to shame the strong. He chose the lowly things of this world and the despised things—and the things that are not—to nullify the things that are, so that no one may boast before him."

Chapter 10

Conclusion

"Christianity, if false, is of no importance, and if true, of infinite importance. The only thing it cannot be is moderately important." - C. S. Lewis

This book was written to assure you of the reasonableness of your Christian faith, as well as to prepare you to reason with others for this truth. Christians who are willing to be used by God to spread the gospel are a significant threat to Satan's kingdom, especially if they have answers to the questions raised by Satan's deceptions. As the father of lies, in this generation Satan has done a tremendous job of attacking the foundations of our faith, especially the book of Genesis. Satan is trying to make the Bible irrelevant and to make life only about the present—and one of his most successful weapons in recent history is the evolution hypothesis.

Whether we know it or not, we are in a spiritual war, and we must be ready to do battle against Satan's delusions at all times. Saying "No, Lord," when called into this battle is the worst oxymoron in the English language; we are left here on earth to be ready to serve! Our attitude should be that of the prophet Isaiah, described in Isaiah 6:8, "Then I heard the voice of the Lord saying, 'Whom shall I send? And who will go for us?' And I said, 'Here am I. Send me!'"

Defending the faith is not a special gift only for certain believers, but a command for all Christians. Always

227

remember 1 Peter 3:15, "But in your hearts revere Christ as Lord. Always be prepared to give an answer to everyone who asks you to give the reason for the hope that you have. But do this with gentleness and respect."

Beliefs have consequences. To illustrate, let's look at Jeffrey Dahmer. He murdered at least 17 men and boys between 1978 and 1991. His murders included unspeakably gruesome acts. He was sentenced to life in prison. There he experienced a huge change in his life and worldview.

When Dahmer was interviewed with his father on Dateline NBC, Nov. 29, 1994 he directed this message to his father: "Thanks to you for sending that creation science material. Because I always believed the lie that evolution is truth, the theory of evolution is truth, that we all just came from the slime, and when we died, you know, that was it, there was nothing—so the whole theory cheapens life. I started reading books that show how evolution is just a complete lie. There's no basis in science to uphold it. And I've since come to believe that the Lord Jesus Christ is the true Creator of the heavens and the earth, which it didn't just happen. I've accepted him as my Lord and Savior, and I believe that I, as well as everyone else will be accountable to him....If a person doesn't think there is a God to be accountable to, then what's the point in trying to modify your behavior to keep it in acceptable ranges? That's how I thought anyway. I've since come to believe that the Lord Jesus Christ is truly God. The Father, the Son, and the Holy Spirit – they are the only true God."

Dahmer was right. The anti-God rebellious worldview that accepts evolution as fact cheapens life. There

228

is no "image of God" that gives value to each person. Evolution has been used to "scientifically" validate many evils in the world including atheism, racism, communism, and Nazism.

Dahmer also illustrates that even the worst of people can receive forgiveness from the Creator God if they put their trust in Jesus. Dahmer was killed in prison nine months after the interview, but now I believe he is in heaven. His story also shows how important it is to reason with people regarding the evidence for God, using creationist material. Dahmer was convinced by reading the evidence for creation. That evidence is more important than ever in this generation as we try to save lost souls and bring a halt to the disastrous consequences resulting from the rebellious worldview. I encourage you to continue to learn more. I encourage you to use the internet. There are resources available like never before to prepare you to spread this truth among your family and friends.

Here's a final word from Charlie Campbell, Director of the Always Be Ready Apologetics Ministry: "Can you imagine an ambassador for your country neglecting to prepare himself for the common questions foreigners ask about his homeland? That would be irresponsible. He'd be without a job very quickly. The Bible tells us that followers of Jesus are His ambassadors to the world (2 Corinthians 5:20). That being the case, it is important that every Christian consider the following questions: Are you ready to answer the common questions people ask about God? Are you ready to explain to someone why you believe the Bible is trustworthy? 1 Peter 3:15 tells us that we are to be ready to give a defense of our faith. Are you ready? Sadly, many Christians watch more television in a week than they'll spend in a year preparing themselves to answer skeptics' and atheists' questions about God and the Bible. Don't leave defending the faith to your pastor. The church needs an army of saints who are able to articulate the truth persuasively and graciously. In Jude 3 we are all called to 'contend earnestly for the faith.' The world needs the gospel! And those who have doubts and questions about our message should be able to find Christians who are able to explain to them the good reasons they should be able to take the Bible and the claims of Jesus seriously."

Made in the USA
Las Vegas, NV
06 December 2023

82216513R00128